Concerning Questions of Leninism
Joseph Stalin

SAI Press
Dickinson, ND.

This edition first published July, 2021.

ISBN-13: 978-1-105-46089-0

Concerning Questions of Leninism

Joseph Stalin

Table of Contents

I. The Definition of Leninism

The pamphlet *The Foundations of Leninism* contains a definition of Leninism which seems to have received general recognition. It runs as follows:

"Leninism is Marxism of the era of imperialism and the proletarian revolution. To be more exact, Leninism is the theory and tactics of the proletarian revolution in general, the theory and tactics of the dictatorship of the proletariat in particular."[1]

Is this definition correct?

I think it is correct. It is correct, firstly, because it correctly indicates the historical roots of Leninism, characterising it as Marxism of the *era of imperialism*, as against certain critics of Lenin who wrongly think that Leninism originated after the imperialist war. It is correct, secondly, because it correctly notes the international character of Leninism, as against Social-Democracy, which considers that Leninism is applicable only to Russian national conditions. It is correct, thirdly, because it correctly notes the organic connection between Leninism and the teachings of Marx, characterising Leninism as *Marxism* of the era of imperialism, as against certain critics of Leninism who consider it not a further development of Marxism, but merely the restoration of Marxism and its application to Russian conditions.

All that, one would think, needs no special comment. Nevertheless, it appears that there are people in our party who consider it necessary to define Leninism somewhat differently. Zinoviev, for example, thinks that:

"Leninism is Marxism of the era of imperialist wars and of the world revolution *which began directly in a country where the peasantry predominates.*"

What can be the meaning of the words underlined by Zinoviev? What does introducing the backwardness of Russia, its peasant character, into the definition of Leninism mean?

It means transforming Leninism from an international proletarian doctrine into a product of specifically Russian conditions.

It means playing into the hands of Bauer and Kautsky, who deny that Leninism is suitable for other countries, for countries in which capitalism is more developed.

It goes without saying that the peasant question is of very great importance for Russia, that our country is a peasant country. But what significance can this fact have in characterising the foundations of Leninism? Was Leninism elaborated only on Russian soil, for Russia alone, and not on the soil of imperialism, and for the imperialist countries generally? Do such works of Lenin as *Imperialism, the Highest Stage of Capitalism*,[2] *The State and Revolution*,[3] *The Proletarian Revolution and the Renegade Kautsky*,[4] "Left-Wing" Communism, an Infantile Disorder,[5] etc., apply only to Russia, and not to all imperialist countries in general? Is not Leninism the generalisation of the experience of the revolutionary movement of *all* countries? Are not the fundamentals of the theory and tactics of Leninism suitable, are they not obligatory, for the proletarian parties of *all* countries? Was not Lenin right when he said that "Bolshevism *can serve as a model of tactics for all*"? (See Vol. XXIII, p. 386.) Was not Lenin right when he spoke about the "*international significance* of Soviet power and of the fundamentals of Bolshevik theory and tactics"? (See Vol. XXV, pp. 171-72.) Are not, for example, the following words of Lenin correct?

"In Russia, the dictatorship of the proletariat must inevitably differ in certain specific features from that in the advanced countries, owing to the very great backwardness and petty-bourgeois character of our country. But the basic forces— and the basic forms of social economy—are the same in Russia as in any capitalist country, so that *these specific features can relate only to what is not most important*" (see Vol. XXIV, p.

8

508).

But if all that is true, does it not follow that Zinoviev's definition of Leninism cannot be regarded as correct?

How can this nationally restricted definition of Leninism be reconciled with internationalism?

II. The Main Thing In Leninism

In the pamphlet *The Foundations of Leninism*, it stated:

"Some think that the fundamental thing in Leninism is the peasant question, that the point of departure of Leninism is the question of the peasantry, of its role, its relative importance. This is absolutely wrong. The fundamental question of Leninism, its point of departure, is not the peasant question, but the question of the dictatorship of the proletariat, of the conditions under which it can be achieved, of the conditions under which it can be consolidated. The peasant question, as the question of the ally of the proletariat in its struggle for power, is a derivative question."[6]

Is this thesis correct?

I think it is correct. This thesis follows entirely from the definition of Leninism. Indeed, if Leninism is the theory and tactics of the proletarian revolution, and the basic content of the proletarian revolution is the dictatorship of the proletariat, then it is clear that the main thing in Leninism is the question of the dictatorship of the proletariat, the elaboration of this question, the substantiation and concretisation of this question.

Nevertheless, Zinoviev evidently does not agree with this thesis. In his article "In Memory of Lenin," he says:

"As I have already said, the question of the role of the peasantry is the *fundamental question* of Bolshevism, of Leninism."

As you see, Zinoviev's thesis follows entirely from his wrong definition of Leninism. It is therefore as wrong as his definition of Leninism is wrong.

Is Lenin's thesis that the dictatorship of the proletariat is the "root content of the proletarian revolution" correct? (See Vol. XXIII, p. 337.) It is unquestionably correct. Is the thesis that Leninism is the theory and tactics of the proletarian revolution correct? I think it is correct. But what follows from this? From this it follows that the fundamental question of Leninism, its point of departure, its foundation, is the question of the dictatorship of the proletariat.

Is it not true that the question of imperialism, the question of the spasmodic character of the development of imperialism, the question of the victory of socialism in one country, the question of the proletarian state, the question of the Soviet form of this state, the question of the role of the Party in the system of the dictatorship of the proletariat, the question of the paths of building socialism—that all these questions were elaborated precisely by Lenin? Is it not true that it is precisely these questions that constitute the basis, the foundation of the idea of the dictatorship of the proletariat? Is it not true that without the elaboration of these fundamental questions, the elaboration of the peasant question from the standpoint of the dictatorship of the proletariat would be inconceivable?

It goes without saying that Lenin was an expert on the peasant question. It goes without saying that the peasant question as the question of the ally of the proletariat is of the greatest significance for the proletariat and forms a constituent part of the fundamental question of the dictatorship of the proletariat. But is it not clear that if Leninism had not been faced with the fundamental question of the dictatorship of the proletariat, the derivative question of the ally of the proletariat, the question of the peasantry, would not have arisen either? Is it not clear that if Leninism had not been faced with the practical question of the conquest of power by the proletariat, the question of an alliance with the peasantry would not have arisen either?

Lenin would not have been the great ideological leader of the proletariat that he unquestionably is—he would have been a simple "peasant philosopher," as foreign literary philistines often depict him—had he elaborated the peasant question, not on the basis of the theory and tactics of the dictatorship of the proletariat, but independently of this basis, apart from this basis.

One or the other:

Either the peasant question is the main thing in Leninism, and in that case Leninism is not suitable, not obligatory, for capitalistically developed countries, for those which are not peasant countries.

Or the main thing in Leninism is the dictatorship of the proletariat, and in that case Leninism is the international doctrine of the proletarians of all lands, suitable and obligatory for all countries without exception, including the capitalistically developed countries.

Here one must choose.

III. The Question of "Permanent" Revolution

In the pamphlet *The Foundations of Leninism*, the "theory of permanent revolution" is appraised as a "theory" which under-estimates the role of the peasantry. There it is stated:

"Consequently, Lenin fought the adherents of 'permanent' revolution, not over the question of uninterruptedness, for Lenin himself maintained the point of view of uninterrupted revolution, but because they under-estimated the role of the peasantry, which is an enormous reserve of the proletariat."[7]

This characterisation of the Russian "permanentists" was considered as generally accepted until recently. Nevertheless, although in general correct, it cannot be regarded as exhaustive. The discussion of 1924, on the one hand, and a careful analysis of the works of Lenin, on the other hand, have shown that the mistake of the Russian "permanentists" lay not only in their under-estimation of the role of the peasantry, but also in their under-estimation of the strength of the proletariat and its capacity to lead the peasantry, in their disbelief in the idea of the hegemony of the proletariat.

That is why, in my pamphlet *The October Revolution and the Tactics of the Russian Communists* (December 1924), I broadened this characterisation and replaced it by another, more complete one. Here is what is stated in that pamphlet:

"Hitherto only one aspect of the theory of 'permanent revolution' has usually been noted—lack of faith in the revolutionary potentialities of the peasant movement. Now, in fairness, this must be supplemented by *another* aspect—lack of faith in the strength and capacity of the proletariat in Russia."[8]

This does not mean, of course, that Leninism has been

13

or is opposed to the idea of permanent revolution, without quotation marks, which was proclaimed by Marx in the forties of the last century.[9] On the contrary, Lenin was the only Marxist who correctly understood and developed the idea of permanent revolution. What distinguishes Lenin from the "permanentists" on this question is that the "permanentists" distorted Marx's idea of permanent revolution and transformed it into lifeless, bookish wisdom, whereas Lenin took it in its pure form and made it one of the foundations of his own theory of revolution. It should be borne in mind that the idea of the growing over of the bourgeois-democratic revolution into the socialist revolution, propounded by Lenin as long ago as 1905, is one of the forms of the embodiment of Marx's theory of permanent revolution. Here is what Lenin wrote about this as far back as 1905:

"From the democratic revolution we shall at once, and just to the extent of our strength, the strength of the class-conscious and organised proletariat, begin to pass to the socialist revolution. *We stand for uninterrupted revolution.* We shall not stop halfway. . . .

"Without succumbing to adventurism or going against our scientific conscience, without striving for cheap popularity, we can and do say *only one thing*: we shall put every effort into assisting the entire peasantry to carry out the democratic revolution *in order thereby to make it easier* for us, the party of the proletariat, to pass on, as quickly as possible, to the new and higher task—the socialist revolution" (see Vol. VIII, pp. 186-87).

And here is what Lenin wrote on this subject sixteen years later, after the conquest of power by the proletariat:

"The Kautskys, Hilferdings, Martovs, Chernovs, Hillquits, Longuets, MacDonalds, Turatis, and other heroes of 'Two-and-a-Half' Marxism were incapable of understanding . . . the relation between the bourgeois-democratic and the proletarian-socialist revolutions. *The first grows over into the*

14

second. The second, in passing, solves the questions of the first. The second consolidates the work of the first. Struggle, and struggle alone, decides how far the second succeeds in outgrowing the first" (see Vol. XXVII, p. 26).

I draw special attention to the first of the above quotations, taken from Lenin's article entitled "The Attitude of Social-Democracy Towards the Peasant Movement," published on September 1, 1905. I emphasise this for the information of those who still continue to assert that Lenin arrived at the idea of the growing over of the bourgeois-democratic revolution into the socialist revolution, that is to say, the idea of permanent revolution, after the imperialist war. This quotation leaves no doubt that these people are profoundly mistaken.

IV. The Proletarian Revolution and the Dictatorship of the Proletariat

What are the characteristic features of the proletarian revolution as distinct from the bourgeois revolution?

The distinction between the proletarian revolution and the bourgeois revolution may be reduced to five main points.

1) The bourgeois revolution usually begins when there already exist more or less ready-made forms belonging to the capitalist order, forms which have grown and matured within the womb of feudal society prior to the open revolution, whereas the proletarian revolution begins when ready-made forms belonging to the socialist order are either absent, or almost absent.

2) The main task of the bourgeois revolution consists in seizing power and making it conform to the already existing bourgeois economy, whereas the main task of the proletarian revolution consists, after seizing power, in building a new, socialist economy.

3) The bourgeois revolution is usually *consummated* with the seizure of power, whereas in the proletarian revolution the seizure of power is only the *beginning*, and power is used as a lever for transforming the old economy and organising the new one.

4) The bourgeois revolution limits itself to replacing one group of exploiters in power by another group of exploiters, in view of which it need not smash the old state machine; whereas the proletarian revolution removes all exploiting groups from power and places in power the leader of all the toilers and exploited, the class of proletarians, in view of which it cannot manage without smashing the old state machine and substituting a now one for it.

5) The bourgeois revolution cannot rally the millions of the toiling and exploited masses around the bourgeoisie for any length of time, for the very reason that they are toilers and exploited; whereas the proletarian revolution can and must link them, precisely as toilers and exploited, in a durable alliance with the proletariat, if it wishes to carry out its main task of consolidating the power of the proletariat and building a new, socialist economy.

Here are some of Lenin's main theses on this subject:

"One of the fundamental differences between bourgeois revolution and socialist revolution," says Lenin, "is that for the bourgeois revolution, which arises out of feudalism, the new economic organisations are gradually created in the womb of the old order, gradually changing all the aspects of feudal society. Bourgeois revolution was confronted by only one task —to sweep away, to cast aside, to destroy all the fetters of the preceding society. By fulfilling this task every bourgeois revolution fulfils all that is required of it: it accelerates the growth of capitalism.

"The socialist revolution is in an altogether different position. The more backward the country which, owing to the zigzags of history, has proved to be the one to start the socialist revolution, the more difficult it is for it to pass from the old capitalist relations to socialist relations. To the tasks of destruction are added new tasks of unprecedented difficulty— organisational tasks" (see Vol. XXII, p. 315).

"Had not the popular creative spirit of the Russian revolution," continues Lenin, "which had gone through the great experience of the year 1905, given rise to the Soviets as early as February 1917, they could not under any circumstances have seized power in October, because success depended entirely upon the existence of ready-made organisational forms of a movement embracing millions. These ready-made forms were the Soviets, and that is why in the political sphere there awaited us those brilliant successes, the continuous triumphant march, that we experienced; for the new form of political power was ready to hand, and all we had to do was, by passing a few decrees, to transform the power of the Soviets from the embryonic state in which it existed in the first months of the revolution into a legally recognised form which has become established in the Russian state—i.e., into the Russian Soviet Republic" (see Vol. XXII, p. 315).

"But two problems of enormous difficulty still remained," says Lenin, "the solution of which could not possibly be the triumphant march which our revolution experienced in the first months . . . " (*ibid.*).

"Firstly, there were the problems of internal organisation, which confront every socialist revolution. The difference between socialist revolution and bourgeois revolution lies precisely in the fact that the latter finds ready-made forms of capitalist relationships, while Soviet power—proletarian power—does not inherit such ready-made relationships, if we leave out of account the most developed forms of capitalism, which, strictly speaking, extended to but a small top layer of industry and hardly touched agriculture. The organisation of accounting, the control of large enterprises, the transformation of the whole of the state economic mechanism into a single huge machine, into an economic organism that works in such a way that hundreds of millions of people are guided by a single plan—such was the enormous organisational problem that rested on our shoulders. Under the present conditions of labour this problem could not possibly be solved by the 'hurrah' methods by which we were able to solve the problems of the Civil War" (*ibid.*, p. 318).

"The second enormous difficulty . . . was the international question. The reason why we were able to cope so easily with Kerensky's gangs, why we so easily established our power and without the slightest difficulty passed the decrees on the socialisation of the land and on workers' control, the reason why we achieved all this so easily was only that a fortunate combination of circumstances protected us for a short time from international imperialism. International imperialism, with the entire might of its capital, with its highly organised military technique, which is a real force, a real fortress of international capital, could in no case, under no circumstances, live side by side with the Soviet Republic, both because of its objective position and because of the economic interests of the capitalist class which is embodied in it—it could not do so because of commercial connections, of international financial relations. In this sphere a conflict is inevitable. Therein lies the greatest difficulty of the Russian revolution, its greatest historical problem: the necessity of solving the international tasks, the necessity of calling forth an international revolution" (see Vol. XXII, p. 317).

Such is the intrinsic character and the basic meaning of the proletarian revolution.

Can such a radical transformation of the old bourgeois order be achieved without a violent revolution, without the dictatorship of the proletariat?

Obviously not. To think that such a revolution can be carried out peacefully, within the framework of bourgeois democracy, which is adapted to the rule of the bourgeoisie, means that one has either gone out of one's mind and lost normal human understanding, or has grossly and openly repudiated the proletarian revolution.

This thesis must be emphasised all the more strongly and categorically for the reason that we are dealing with the proletarian revolution which for the time being has triumphed only in one country, a country which is surrounded by hostile capitalist countries and the bourgeoisie of which cannot fail to receive the support of international capital.

That is why Lenin says that:

"The emancipation of the oppressed class is impossible not only without a violent revolution, *but also without the destruction* of the apparatus of state power which was created by the ruling class" (see Vol. XXI, p. 373).

"First let the majority of the population, while private property still exists, i.e., while the rule and yoke of capital still exists, express themselves in favour of the party of the proletariat, and only then can and should the party take power— *so say the petty-bourgeois democrats who call themselves 'Socialists' but who are in reality the servitors of the bourgeoisie*" (see Vol. XXIV, p. 647).

"*We say*: Let the revolutionary proletariat first overthrow the bourgeoisie, break the yoke of capital, and smash the bourgeois state apparatus, then the victorious proletariat will be able rapidly to gain the sympathy and support of the majority of the toiling non-proletarian masses by satisfying their needs at the expense of the exploiters" (*ibid.*).

"In order to win the majority of the population to its side," Lenin says further, "the proletariat must, in the first place, overthrow the bourgeoisie and seize state power; secondly, it must introduce Soviet power and smash the old state apparatus to bits, whereby it immediately undermines the rule, prestige and influence of the bourgeoisie and petty-bourgeois compromisers over the non-proletarian toiling masses. Thirdly, it must *entirely destroy* the influence of the bourgeoisie and petty-bourgeois compromisers over the *majority* of the non-proletarian toiling masses by satisfying their economic needs *in a revolutionary way at the expense of the exploiters*" (*ibid.*, p. 641).

Such are the characteristic features of the proletarian revolution.

What, in this connection, are the main features of the dictatorship of the proletariat, once it is admitted that the dictatorship of the proletariat is the basic content of the proletarian revolution?

Here is the most general definition of the dictatorship of

the proletariat given by Lenin:

"The dictatorship of the proletariat is not the end of the class struggle, but its continuation in new forms. The dictatorship of the proletariat is the class struggle of the proletariat, which has won victory and has seized political power, against the bourgeoisie, which although vanquished has not been annihilated, has not disappeared, has not ceased its resistance, has increased its resistance" (see Vol. XXIV, p. 311).

Arguing against confusing the dictatorship of the proletariat with "popular" government, "elected by all," with "non-class" government, Lenin says:

"The class which took political power into its hands did so knowing that it took power alone. That is a part of the concept dictatorship of the proletariat. This concept has meaning only when this one class knows that it alone is taking political power in its hands, and does not deceive itself or others with talk about 'popular' government, 'elected by all, sanctified by the whole people'" (see Vol. XXVI, p. 286).

This does not mean, however, that the power of one class, the class of the proletarians, which does not and cannot share power with other classes, does not need aid from, and an alliance with, the labouring and exploited masses of other classes for the achievement of its aims. On the contrary. This power, the power of one class, can be firmly established and exercised to the full only by means of a special form of alliance between the class of proletarians and the labouring masses of the petty-bourgeois classes, primarily the labouring masses of the peasantry.

What is this special form of alliance? What does it consist in? Does not this alliance with the labouring masses of other, non-proletarian, classes wholly contradict the idea of the dictatorship of one class?

This special form of alliance consists in that the guiding force of this alliance is the proletariat. This special form of

21

alliance consists in that the leader of the state, the leader in the system of the dictatorship of the proletariat is *one* party, the party of the proletariat, the Party of the Communists, which *does not and cannot share* leadership with other parties.

As you see, the contradiction is only an apparent, a seeming one.

"The dictatorship of the proletariat," says Lenin, "is *a special form of class alliance* between the proletariat, the vanguard of the working people, and the numerous non-proletarian strata of working people (the petty bourgeoisie, the small proprietors, the peasantry, the intelligentsia, etc.), or the majority of these; it is an alliance against capital, an alliance aiming at the complete overthrow of capital, at the complete suppression of the resistance of the bourgeoisie and of any attempt on its part at restoration, an alliance aiming at the final establishment and consolidation of socialism. It is a special type of alliance, which is being built up in special circumstances, namely, in the circumstances of fierce civil war; it is an alliance of the firm supporters of socialism with the latter's wavering allies and sometimes with 'neutrals' (then instead of an agreement for struggle, the alliance becomes an agreement for neutrality), *an alliance between classes which differ economically, politically, socially and ideologically*" (see Vol. XXIV, p. 311).

In one of his instructional reports, Kamenev, disputing this conception of the dictatorship of the proletariat, states:

"The dictatorship *is not* an alliance of one class with another."

I believe that Kamenev here has in view, primarily, a passage in my pamphlet *The October Revolution and the Tactics of the Russian Communists*, where it is stated:

"The dictatorship of the proletariat is not simply a governmental top stratum 'skilfully' 'selected' by the careful hand of an 'experienced strategist,' and 'judiciously relying' on the support of one section or another of the population. The dictatorship of the proletariat is the class alliance between the proletariat and the labouring masses of the peasantry for the purpose of overthrowing capital, for achieving the final victory of socialism, on the condition that the guiding force of this alliance is the proletariat."[10]

I wholly endorse this formulation of the dictatorship of the proletariat, for I think that it fully and entirely coincides with Lenin's formulation, just quoted.

I assert that Kamenev's statement that "the dictatorship *is not* an alliance of one class with another," in the categorical form in which it is made, has nothing in common with Lenin's theory of the dictatorship of the proletariat.

I assert that such statements can be made only by people who have failed to understand the meaning of the idea of the bond, the idea of the alliance of the proletariat and peasantry, the idea of the *hegemony* of the proletariat within this alliance.

Such statements can be made only by people who have failed to understand Lenin's thesis:

"*Only an agreement with the peasantry* can save the socialist revolution in Russia as long as the revolution in other countries has not taken place" (see Vol. XXVI, p. 238).

Such statements can be made only by people who have failed to understand Lenin's thesis:

"*The supreme principle of the dictatorship* is the maintenance of the alliance of the proletariat and peasantry in order that the proletariat may retain its leading role and state power" (*ibid.*, p. 460).

Pointing out one of the most important aims of the dictatorship, the aim of suppressing the exploiters, Lenin says:

"The scientific concept of dictatorship means nothing more nor less than completely unrestricted power, absolutely unimpeded by laws or regulations and resting directly on the

23

use of force" (see Vol. XXV, p. 441).

"Dictatorship means—note this once and for all, Messrs. Cadets—unrestricted power, based on force and not on law. In time of civil war any victorious power can be only a dictatorship" (see Vol. XXV, p. 436).

But of course, the dictatorship of the proletariat does not mean only the use of force, although there is no dictatorship without the use of force.

"Dictatorship," says Lenin, "does not mean only the use of force, although it is impossible without the use of force; it also means the organisation of labour on a higher level than the previous organisation" (see Vol. XXIV, p. 305).

"The dictatorship of the proletariat . . . is not only the use of force against the exploiters, and not even mainly the use of force. The economic foundation of this revolutionary use of force, the guarantee of its effectiveness and success is the fact that the proletariat represents and creates a higher type of social organisation of labour compared with capitalism. This is the essence. This is the source of the strength and the guarantee of the inevitable complete triumph of communism" (see Vol. XXIV, pp. 335-36).

"Its quintessence (i.e., of the dictatorship—*J. St.*) is the organisation and discipline of the advanced detachment of the working people, of its vanguard, its sole leader, the proletariat, whose object is to build socialism, to abolish the division of society into classes, to make all members of society working people, to remove the basis for any exploitation of man by man. This object cannot be achieved at one stroke. It requires a fairly long period of transition from capitalism to socialism, because the reorganisation of production is a difficult matter, because radical changes in all spheres of life need time, and because the enormous force of habit of petty-bourgeois and bourgeois conduct of economy can be overcome only by a long and stubborn struggle. That is why Marx spoke of an entire period of the dictatorship of the proletariat, as the period of transition from capitalism to socialism" (*ibid.*, p. 314).

Such are the characteristic features of the dictatorship of the proletariat.

Hence the three main aspects of the dictatorship of the proletariat.

1) The utilisation of the rule of the proletariat for the suppression of the exploiters, for the defence of the country, for the consolidation of the ties with the proletarians of other lands, and for the development and victory of the revolution in all countries.

2) The utilisation of the rule of the proletariat in order to detach the labouring and exploited masses once and for all from the bourgeoisie, to consolidate the alliance of the proletariat with these masses, to draw these masses into the work of socialist construction, and to ensure the state leadership of these masses by the proletariat.

3) The utilisation of the rule of the proletariat for the organisation of socialism, for the abolition of classes, for the transition to a society without classes, to a socialist society.

The proletarian dictatorship is a combination of all these three aspects. No single one of these aspects can be advanced as the *sole* characteristic feature of the dictatorship of the proletariat. On the other hand, in the circumstances of capitalist encirclement, the absence of even one of these features is sufficient for the dictatorship of the proletariat to cease being a dictatorship. Therefore, not one of these three aspects can be omitted without running the risk of distorting the concept of the dictatorship of the proletariat. Only all these three aspects taken together give us the complete and finished concept of the dictatorship of the proletariat.

The dictatorship of the proletariat has its periods, its special forms, diverse methods of work. During the period of civil war, it is the forcible aspect of the dictatorship that is most conspicuous. But it by no means follows from this that no constructive work is carried on during the period of civil war. Without constructive work it is impossible to wage civil war. During the period of socialist construction, on the other hand, it is the peaceful, organisational and cultural work of the dictatorship, revolutionary law, etc., that are most conspicuous. But, again, it by no means follows from this that the forcible aspect of the dictatorship has ceased to exist or can cease to exist in the period of construction. The organs of suppression, the army and other organisations, are as necessary now, at the time of construction, as they were during the period of civil war. Without these organs, constructive work by the dictatorship with any degree of security would be impossible. It should not be forgotten that for the time being the revolution has been victorious in only one country. It should not be forgotten that as long as capitalist encirclement exists the danger of intervention, with all the consequences resulting from this danger, will also exist.

V. The Party and the Working Class in the System of the Dictatorship of the Proletariat

I have dealt above with the dictatorship of the proletariat from the point of view of its historical inevitability, from the point of view of its class content, from the point of view of its state nature, and, finally, from the point of view of the destructive and creative tasks which it performs throughout the entire historical period that is termed the period of transition from capitalism to socialism.

Now we must say something about the dictatorship of the proletariat from the point of view of its structure, from the point of view of its "mechanism," from the point of view of the role and significance of the "transmission belts," the "levers," and the "directing force" which in their totality constitute "the system of the dictatorship of the proletariat" (*Lenin*), and with the help of which the daily work of the dictatorship of the proletariat is accomplished.

What are these "transmission belts" or "levers" in the system of the dictatorship of the proletariat? What is this "directing force"? Why are they needed?

The levers or transmission belts are those very mass organisations of the proletariat without the aid of which the dictatorship cannot be realised.

The directing force is the advanced detachment of the proletariat, its vanguard, which is the main guiding force of the dictatorship of the proletariat.

The proletariat needs these transmission belts, these levers, and this directing force, because without them, in its struggle for victory, it would be a weaponless army in face of organised and armed capital. The proletariat needs these organisations because without them it would suffer inevitable defeat in its fight for the overthrow of the bourgeoisie, in its fight for the consolidation of its rule, in its fight for the building of socialism. The systematic help of these organisations and the directing force of the vanguard are needed because in the absence of these conditions it is impossible for the dictatorship of the proletariat to be at all durable and firm.

What are these organisations?

Firstly, there are the workers' *trade unions*, with their central and local ramifications in the shape of a whole series of organisations concerned with production, culture, education, etc. These unite the workers of all trades. They are non-Party organisations. The trade unions may be termed the all-embracing organisation of the working class, which is in power in our country. They are a school of communism. They promote the best people from their midst for the work of leadership in all branches of administration. They form the link between the advanced and the backward elements in the ranks of the working class. They connect the masses of the workers with the vanguard of the working class.

Secondly, there are the *Soviets*, with their numerous central and local ramifications in the shape of administrative, economic, military, cultural and other state organisations, plus the innumerable mass associations of the working people which have sprung up of their own accord and which encompass these organisations and connect them with the population. The Soviets are a mass organisation of all the working people of town and country. They are a non-Party organisation. The Soviets are the direct expression of the dictatorship of the proletariat. It is through the Soviets that all measures for strengthening the dictatorship and for building socialism are carried out. It is through the Soviets that the state leadership of the peasantry by the proletariat is exercised. The Soviets connect the vast masses of the working people with the vanguard of the proletariat.

28

Thirdly, there are the *co-operatives* of all kinds, with all their ramifications. These are a mass organisation of the working people, a non-Party organisation, which unites the working people primarily as consumers, and also, in the course of time, as producers (agricultural co-operatives). The co-operatives acquire special significance after the consolidation of the dictatorship of the proletariat, during the period of extensive construction. They facilitate contact between the vanguard of the proletariat and the mass of the peasantry and make it possible to draw the latter into the channel of socialist construction.

Fourthly, there is the *Youth League*. This is a mass organisation of young workers and peasants; it is a non-Party organisation, but is linked with the Party. Its task is to help the Party to educate the young generation in the spirit of socialism. It provides young reserves for all the other mass organisations of the proletariat in all branches of administration. The Youth League has acquired special significance since the consolidation of the dictatorship of the proletariat, in the period of extensive cultural and educational work carried on by the proletariat.

Lastly, there is the *Party* of the proletariat, its vanguard. Its strength lies in the fact that it draws into its ranks all the best elements of the proletariat from all the mass organisations of the latter. Its function is to *combine* the work of all the mass organisations of the proletariat without exception and to *direct* their activities towards a single goal, the goal of the emancipation of the proletariat. And it is absolutely necessary to combine and direct them towards a single goal, for otherwise unity in the struggle of the proletariat is impossible, for otherwise the guidance of the proletarian masses in their struggle for power, in their struggle for building socialism, is impossible. But, only the vanguard of the proletariat, its Party, is capable of combining and directing the work of the mass organisations of the proletariat. Only the Party of the proletariat, only the Communist Party, is capable of fulfilling this role of main leader in the system of the dictatorship of the proletariat.

Why?

"... because, in the first place, it is the rallying centre of the finest elements in the working class, who have direct connections with the non-Party organisations of the proletariat and very frequently lead them; because, secondly, the Party, as the rallying centre of the finest members of the working class, is the best school for training leaders of the working class, capable of directing every form of organisation of their class; because, thirdly, the Party, as the best school for training leaders of the working class, is, by reason of its experience and prestige, the only organisation capable of centralising the leadership of the struggle of the proletariat, thus transforming each and every non-Party organisation of the working class into an auxiliary body and transmission belt linking the Party with the class" (see *The Foundations of Leninism*[11]).

The Party is the main guiding force in the system of the dictatorship of the proletariat.

"The Party is the highest form of class organisation of the proletariat" (*Lenin*).

To sum up: the *trade unions*, as the mass organisation of the proletariat, linking the Party with the class primarily in the sphere of production; the *Soviets*, as the mass organisation of the working people, linking the Party with the latter primarily in the sphere of state administration; the *co-operatives*, as the mass organisation mainly of the peasantry, linking the Party with the peasant masses primarily in the economic sphere, in the sphere of drawing the peasantry into the work of socialist construction; the *Youth League*, as the mass organisation of young workers and peasants, whose mission it is to help the vanguard of the proletariat in the socialist education of the new generation and in training young reserves; and, finally, the *Party*, as the main directing force in the system of the dictatorship of the proletariat, whose mission it is to lead all these mass organisations—such, in general, is the picture of the "mechanism" of the dictatorship, the picture of "the system of

30

the dictatorship of the proletariat."

Without the Party as the main guiding force, it is impossible for the dictatorship of the proletariat to be at all durable and firm.

Thus, in the words of Lenin, "taken as a whole, we have a formally non-communist, flexible and relatively wide, and very powerful proletarian apparatus, by means of which the Party is closely linked with the *class* and with the *masses*, and by means of which, under the leadership of the Party, the *dictatorship of the class* is exercised" (see Vol. XXV, p. 192).

Of course, this must not be understood in the sense that the Party can or should take the place of the trade unions, the Soviets, and the other mass organisations. The Party exercises the dictatorship of the proletariat. However, it exercises it not directly, but with the help of the trade unions, and through the Soviets and their ramifications. Without these "transmission belts," it would be impossible for the dictatorship to be at all firm.

"It is impossible to exercise the dictatorship," says Lenin, "without having a number of 'transmission belts' from the vanguard to the mass of the advanced class, and from the latter to the mass of the working people" (see Vol. XXVI, p. 65).

"The Party, so to speak, draws into its ranks the vanguard of the proletariat, and this vanguard exercises the dictatorship of the proletariat. Without a foundation like the trade unions the dictatorship cannot be exercised, state functions cannot be fulfilled. And these functions have to be exercised *through* a number of special institutions also of a new type; namely, *through* the Soviet apparatus" (see Vol. XXVI, p. 64).

The highest expression of the leading role of the Party, here, in the Soviet Union, in the land of the dictatorship of the proletariat, for example, is the fact that not a single important political or organisational question is decided by our Soviet and other mass organisations without guiding directives from the Party. *In this sense* it could be said that the dictatorship of the proletariat is, *in essence*, the "dictatorship" of its vanguard, the "dictatorship" of its Party, as the main guiding force of the proletariat. Here is what Lenin said on this subject at the Second Congress of the Comintern [12]:

"Tanner says that he stands for the dictatorship of the proletariat, but the dictatorship of the proletariat is not conceived quite in the same way as we conceive it. He says that by the dictatorship of the proletariat we mean, *in essence*, the dictatorship of its organised and class-conscious minority.

"And, as a matter of fact, in the era of capitalism, when the masses of the workers are continuously subjected to exploitation and cannot develop their human potentialities, the most characteristic feature of working-class political parties is that they can embrace only a minority of their class. A political party can comprise only a minority of the class, in the same way as the really class-conscious workers in every capitalist society constitute only a minority of all the workers. That is why we must admit that only this class-conscious minority can guide the broad masses of the workers and lead them. And if Comrade Tanner says that he is opposed to parties, but at the same time is in favour of the minority consisting of the best organised and most revolutionary workers showing the way to the whole of the proletariat, then I say that there is really no difference between us" (see Vol. XXV, p. 347).

But this, however, must not be understood in the sense that a *sign of equality* can be put between the dictatorship of the proletariat and the leading role of the Party (the "dictatorship" of the Party), that the former can be *identified* with the latter, that the latter can be substituted for the former. Sorin, for example, says that "*the dictatorship of the proletariat is the dictatorship of our Party.*" This thesis, as you see, identifies the "dictatorship of the Party" with the dictatorship of the proletariat. Can we regard this identification as correct and yet remain on the ground of Leninism? No, we cannot. And for the following reasons:

Firstly. In the passage from his speech, at the Second Congress of the Comintern quoted above, Lenin does not by any means identify the leading role of the Party with the dictatorship of the proletariat. He merely says that "only this class-conscious minority (i.e., the Party—*J. St.*) can guide the broad masses of the workers and lead them," that it is *precisely in this sense* that "by the dictatorship of the proletariat we mean, *in essence*, the dictatorship of its organised and class-conscious minority."

To say "in essence" does not mean "wholly." We often say that the national question is, in essence, a peasant question. And this is quite true. But this does not mean that the national question is covered by the peasant question, that the peasant question is equal in scope to the national question, that the peasant question and the national question are identical. There is no need to prove that the national question is wider and richer in its scope than the peasant question. The same must be said by analogy as regards the leading role of the Party and the dictatorship of the proletariat. Although the Party carries out the dictatorship of the proletariat, and in this sense the dictatorship of the proletariat is, *in essence*, the "dictatorship" of its Party, this does not mean that the "dictatorship of the Party" (its leading role) is *identical* with the dictatorship of the proletariat, that the former is equal in scope to the latter. There is no need to prove that the dictatorship of the proletariat is wider and richer in its scope than the leading role of the Party. The Party carries out the dictatorship of the proletariat, but it carries out the dictatorship of the *proletariat*, and not any other kind of dictatorship. Whoever identifies the leading role of the Party with the dictatorship of the proletariat substitutes "dictatorship" of the Party for the dictatorship of the proletariat.

Secondly. Not a single important decision is arrived at by the mass organisations of the proletariat without guiding directives from the Party. That is perfectly true. But does that

33

mean that the dictatorship of the proletariat *consists entirely* of the guiding directives given by the Party? Does that mean that, in view of this, the guiding directives of the Party can be identified with the dictatorship of the proletariat? Of course not. The dictatorship of the proletariat consists of the guiding directives of the Party plus the carrying out of these directives by the mass organisations of the proletariat, plus their fulfilment by the population. Here, as you see, we have to deal with a whole series of transitions and intermediary steps which are by no means unimportant elements of the dictatorship of the proletariat. Hence, between the guiding directives of the Party and their fulfilment lie the will and actions of those who are led, the will and actions of the class, its willingness (or unwillingness) to support such directives, its ability (or inability) to carry out these directives, its ability (or inability) to carry them out in strict accordance with the demands of the situation. It scarcely needs proof that the Party, having taken the leadership into its hands, cannot but reckon with the will, the condition, the level of political consciousness of those who are led, cannot leave out of account the will, the condition, and level of political consciousness of its class. Therefore, whoever identifies the leading role of the Party with the dictatorship of the proletariat substitutes the directives given by the Party for the will and actions of the class.

Thirdly. "The dictatorship of the proletariat," says Lenin, "is the class struggle of the proletariat, which has won victory and has seized political power" (see Vol. XXIV, p. 311). How can this *class* struggle find expression? It may find expression in a series of armed actions by the proletariat against the sorties of the overthrown bourgeoisie, or against the intervention of the foreign bourgeoisie. It may find expression in civil war, if the power of the proletariat has not yet been consolidated. It may find expression, after power has already been consolidated, in the extensive organisational and constructive work of the proletariat, with the enlistment of the broad masses in this work. In all these cases, the acting force is the proletariat as *a class*. It has never happened that the Party, the Party alone, has undertaken all these actions with only its own forces, without the support of the class. Usually it only directs these actions, and it can direct them only to the extent that it has the support of the class. For the Party cannot cover, cannot replace the class. For, despite all its important leading role, the Party still remains *a part* of the class. Therefore, whoever identifies the leading role of the Party with the dictatorship of the proletariat substitutes the Party for the class.

Fourthly. The Party exercises the dictatorship of the proletariat. "The Party is the direct governing vanguard of the proletariat; it is the leader" (*Lenin*).[13] In this sense the Party *takes* power, the Party *governs the country*. But this must not be understood in the sense that the Party exercises the dictatorship of the proletariat separately from the state power, without the state power; that the Party governs the country separately from the Soviets, not through the Soviets. This does not mean that the Party can be identified with the Soviets, with the state power. The Party is the core of this power, but it is not and cannot be identified with the state power.

"As the ruling Party," says Lenin, "we could not but merge the Soviet 'top leadership' with the Party 'top leadership'—in our country they are merged and will remain so" (see Vol. XXVI, p. 208). This is quite true. But by this Lenin by no means wants to imply that our Soviet institutions as a whole, for instance our army, our transport, our economic institutions, etc., are Party institutions, that the Party can replace the Soviets and their ramifications, that the Party can be identified with the state power. Lenin repeatedly said that "the system of Soviets is the dictatorship of the proletariat," and that "the Soviet power is the dictatorship of the proletariat" (see Vol. XXIV, pp. 15, 14); but he never said that the Party is the state power, that the Soviets and the Party are one and the same thing. The Party, with a membership of several hundred thousand, guides the Soviets and their central and local ramifications, which embrace tens of millions of people, both

35

Party and non-Party, but it cannot and should not supplant them. That is why Lenin says that "the dictatorship is exercised by the proletariat organised in the Soviets, the proletariat led by the Communist Party of Bolsheviks"; that "all the work of the Party is carried on *through* the Soviets, which embrace the labouring masses irrespective of occupation" (see Vol. XXV, pp. 192, 193); and that the dictatorship "has to be exercised . . . *through* the Soviet apparatus" (see Vol. XXVl, p. 64). Therefore, whoever identifies the leading role of the Party with the dictatorship of the proletariat substitutes the Party for the Soviets, i.e., for the state power.

Fifthly. The concept of dictatorship of the proletariat is a state concept. The dictatorship of the proletariat necessarily includes the concept of force. There is no dictatorship without the use of force, if dictatorship is to be understood in the strict sense of the word. Lenin defines the dictatorship of the proletariat as "power based directly on the *use of force*" (see Vol. XIX, p. 315). Hence, to talk about dictatorship of the Party in *relation to the proletarian class*, and to identify it with the dictatorship of the proletariat, is tantamount to saying that in relation to its class the Party must be not only a guide, not only a leader and teacher, but also a sort of dictator employing force against it, which, of course, is quite incorrect. Therefore, whoever identifies "dictatorship of the Party" with the dictatorship of the proletariat tacitly proceeds from the assumption that the prestige of the Party can be built up on force employed against the working class, which is absurd and quite incompatible with Leninism. The prestige of the Party is sustained by the confidence of the working class. And the confidence of the working class is gained not by force—force only kills it—but by the Party's correct theory, by the Party's correct policy, by the Party's devotion to the working class, by its connection with the masses of the working class, by its readiness and ability to *convince* the masses of the correctness of its slogans.

What, then, follows from all this?

From this it follows that:

1) Lenin uses the word *dictatorship* of the Party not in the strict sense of the word ("power based on the use of force"), but in the figurative sense, in the sense of its undivided leadership.

2) Whoever identifies the leadership of the Party with the *dictatorship* of the proletariat distorts Lenin, wrongly attributing to the Party the function of employing force against the working class as a whole.

3) Whoever attributes to the Party the function, which it does not possess, of employing force against the working class as a whole, violates the elementary requirements of correct mutual relations between the vanguard and the class, between the Party and the proletariat.

Thus, we have come right up to the question of the mutual relations between the Party and the class, between Party and non-Party members of the working class.

Lenin defines these mutual relations as *"mutual confidence* between the vanguard of the working class and the mass of the workers" (see Vol. XXVI, p. 235).

What does this mean?

It means, firstly, that the Party must closely heed the voice of the masses; that it must pay careful attention to the revolutionary instinct of the masses; that it must study the practice of the struggle of the masses and on this basis test the correctness of its own policy; that, consequently, it must not only teach the masses, but also learn from them. It means, secondly, that the Party must day by day win the confidence of the proletarian masses; that it must by its policy and work secure the support of the masses; that it must not command but primarily convince the masses, helping them to realise through their own experience the correctness of the policy of the Party; that, consequently, it must be the guide, the leader and teacher of its class.

To violate these conditions means to upset the correct mutual relations between the vanguard and the class, to undermine "mutual confidence," to shatter both class and Party discipline.

"Certainly," says Lenin, "almost everyone now realises that the Bolsheviks could not have maintained themselves in power for two-and-a-half months, let alone two-and-a-half years, without the strictest, truly iron discipline in our Party, and *without the fullest and unreserved support of the latter by the whole mass of the working class*, that is, by all its thinking, honest, self-sacrificing and influential elements, capable of leading or of carrying with them the backward strata" (see Vol. XXV, p. 173).

"The dictatorship of the proletariat," says Lenin further, "is a stubborn struggle—bloody and bloodless, violent and peaceful, military and economic, educational and administrative —against the forces and traditions of the old society. The force of habit of millions and tens of millions is a most terrible force. Without an iron party tempered in the struggle, without a party *enjoying the confidence of all that is honest in the given class*, without a party capable of watching and influencing the mood of the masses, it is impossible to conduct such a struggle successfully" (see Vol. XXV, p. 190).

But how does the Party acquire this confidence and support of the class? How is the iron discipline necessary for the dictatorship of the proletariat built up within the working class; on what soil does it grow up?

Here is what Lenin says on this subject:

"How is the discipline of the revolutionary party of the proletariat maintained? How is it tested? How is it reinforced? Firstly, by the class consciousness of the proletarian vanguard and by its devotion to the revolution, by its stamina, self-sacrifice and heroism. Secondly, by its ability to link itself with, to keep in close touch with, and to a certain extent, if you like, *to merge with the broadest masses of the working people*—primarily with the proletarian, *but also with the non-proletarian,* labouring masses. Thirdly, by the correctness of the political leadership exercised by this vanguard, by the correctness of its political strategy and tactics, provided that the broadest masses have been convinced *through their own experience* of this correctness. Without these conditions, discipline in a revolutionary party that is really capable of being the party of the advanced class, whose mission it is to overthrow the bourgeoisie and transform the whole of society, cannot be achieved. Without these conditions, attempts to establish discipline inevitably become a cipher, an empty phrase, mere affectation. On the other hand, these conditions cannot arise all at once. They are created only by prolonged effort and hard-won experience. Their creation is facilitated only by correct revolutionary theory, which, in its turn, is not a dogma, but assumes final shape only in close connection with the practical activity of a truly mass and truly revolutionary movement" (see Vol. XXV, p. 174).

And further:

"Victory over capitalism requires the correct correlation between the leading, Communist, Party, the revolutionary class —the proletariat—and the masses, i.e., the working people and exploited as a whole. Only the Communist Party, if it is really the vanguard of the revolutionary class, if it contains all the best representatives of that class, if it consists of fully class-conscious and devoted Communists who have been educated and steeled by the experience of stubborn revolutionary struggle, if this Party has succeeded in linking itself inseparably with the whole life of its class and, through it, with the whole mass of exploited, and if it has succeeded in inspiring the *complete confidence* of this class and *this mass*—only such a party is capable of leading the proletariat in the most ruthless, resolute and final struggle against all the forces of capitalism. On the other hand, only under the leadership of such a party can the proletariat develop the full might of its revolutionary onslaught and nullify the inevitable apathy and, partly, resistance of the small minority of the labour aristocracy corrupted by capitalism, and of the old trade-union and cooperative leaders, etc.—only then will it be able to display its full strength, which, owing to the very economic structure of capitalist society, is immeasurably greater than the proportion of the population it Constitutes" (see Vol. XXV, p. 315).

From these quotations it follows that:

1) The prestige of the Party and the iron discipline within the working class that are necessary for the dictatorship of the proletariat are built up not on fear or on "unrestricted" rights of the Party, but on the confidence of the working class in the Party, on the support which the Party receives from the working class.

2) The confidence of the working class in the Party is not acquired at one stroke, and not by means of force against the working class, but by the Party's prolonged work among the masses, by the correct policy of the Party, by the ability of the Party to convince the masses through their own experience of the correctness of its policy, by the ability of the Party to secure the support of the working class and to take the lead of the masses of the working class.

3) Without a correct Party policy, reinforced by the experience of the struggle of the masses, and without the confidence of the working class, there is not and cannot be real leadership by the Party.

4) The Party and its leadership, if the Party enjoys the confidence of the class, and if this leadership is real leadership, cannot be counterposed to the dictatorship of the proletariat, because without the leadership of the Party (the "dictatorship" of the Party), enjoying the confidence of the working class, it is impossible for the dictatorship of the proletariat to be at all firm.

Without these conditions, the prestige of the Party and iron discipline within the working class are either empty phrases or boastfulness and adventurism.

It is impossible to counterpose the dictatorship of the proletariat to the leadership (the "dictatorship") of the Party. It is impossible because the leadership of the Party is the principal thing in the dictatorship of the proletariat, if we have in mind a dictatorship that is at all firm and complete, and not one like the Paris Commune, for instance, which was neither a complete nor a firm dictatorship. It is impossible because the dictatorship of the proletariat and the leadership of the Party lie, as it were, on the same line of activity, operate in the same direction.

"The mere presentation of the question," says Lenin, "'dictatorship of the Party *or* dictatorship of the class? dictatorship (Party) of the leaders *or* dictatorship (Party) of the masses?' testifies to the most incredible and hopeless confusion of thought. . . . Everyone knows that the masses are divided into classes. . . ; that usually, and in the majority of cases, at least in modern civilised countries, classes are led by political parties; that political parties, as a general rule, are directed by more or less stable groups composed of the most authoritative, influential and experienced members, who are elected to the most responsible positions and are called leaders. . . . To go so far . . . as to counterpose, in general, dictatorship of the masses to dictatorship of the leaders is ridiculously absurd and stupid" (see Vol. XXV, pp. 187, 188).

That is absolutely correct. But that correct statement proceeds from the premise that, correct mutual relations exist between the vanguard and the masses of the workers, between the Party and the class. It proceeds from the assumption that the mutual relations between the vanguard and the class remain, so to say, normal, remain within the bounds of "mutual confidence."

But what if the correct mutual relations between the vanguard and the class, the relations of "mutual confidence" between the Party and the class are upset?

41

What if the Party itself begins, in some way or other, to counterpose itself to the class, thus upsetting the foundations of its correct mutual relations with the class, thus upsetting the foundations of "mutual confidence"? Are such cases at all possible?

Yes, they are.

They are possible:

1) *if* the Party begins to build its prestige among the masses, not on its work and on the confidence of the masses, but on its "unrestricted" rights;

2) *if* the Party's policy is obviously wrong and the Party is unwilling to reconsider and rectify its mistake;

3) *if* the Party's policy is correct on the whole but, the masses are not yet ready to make it their own, and the Party is either unwilling or unable to bide its time so as to give the masses an opportunity to become convinced through their own experience that the Party's policy is correct, and seeks to impose it on the masses.

The history of our Party provides a number of such cases. Various groups and factions in our Party have come to grief and disappeared because they violated one of these three conditions, and sometimes all these conditions taken together.

But it follows from this that counterposing the dictatorship of the proletariat to the "dictatorship" (leadership) of the Party can be regarded as incorrect only:

1) *if* by dictatorship of the Party in relation to the working class we mean not a dictatorship in the proper sense of the word ("power based on the use of force"), but the leadership of the Party, which precludes the use of force against the working class as a whole, against its majority, precisely as Lenin meant it;

2) *if* the Party has the qualifications to be the real leader of the class, i.e., if the Party's policy is correct, if this policy

42

accords with the interests of the class;

3) *if* the class, if the majority of the class, accepts that policy, makes that policy its own, becomes convinced, as a result of the work of the Party, that that policy is correct, has confidence in the Party and supports it.

The violation of these conditions inevitably gives rise to a conflict between the Party and the class, to a split between them, to their being counterposed to each other.

Can the Party's leadership be imposed on the class by force? No, it cannot. At all events, *such* a leadership cannot be at all durable. If the Party wants to remain the Party of the proletariat it must know that it is, primarily and principally, the *guide*, the *leader*, the *teacher* of the working class. We must not forget what Lenin said on this subject in his pamphlet *The State and Revolution*:

"By educating the workers' party, Marxism educates the vanguard of the proletariat, which is capable of taking power and *of leading the whole people* to socialism, of directing and organising the new order, of being the *teacher*, the *guide*, the *leader* of all the toilers and exploited in building up their social life without the bourgeoisie and against the bourgeoisie" (see Vol. XXI, p. 386).

Can one consider the Party as the real leader of the class if its policy is wrong, if its policy comes into collision with the interests of the class? Of course not. In such cases the Party, if it wants to remain the leader, must reconsider its policy, must correct its policy, must acknowledge its mistake and correct it. In confirmation of this thesis one could cite, for example, such a fact from the history of our Party as the period of the abolition of the surplus-appropriation system, when the masses of workers and peasants were obviously discontented with our policy and when the Party openly and honestly decided to reconsider this policy. Here is what Lenin said at the time, at the Tenth Party Congress, on the question of abolishing the surplus-appropriation system and introducing the New Economic Policy:

"We must not try to conceal anything, but must say straightforwardly that the peasantry is not satisfied with the form of relations that has been established with it, that it does not want this form of relations and will not go on living in this way. That is indisputable. It has definitely expressed this will. This is the will of the vast mass of the labouring population. We must reckon with this; and we are sufficiently sober politicians to say straightforwardly: *Let us reconsider our policy towards the peasantry*" (see Vol. XXVI, p. 238).

Can one consider that the Party should take the initiative and leadership in organising decisive actions by the masses merely on the ground that its policy is correct on the whole, *if* that policy does not yet meet the confidence and support of the class because, say, of the latter's political backwardness; *if* the Party has not yet succeeded in convincing the class of the correctness of its policy because, say, events have not yet matured? No, one cannot. In such cases the Party, if it, wants to be a real leader, must know how to bide its time, must convince the masses that its policy is correct, must help the masses to become convinced through their own experience that this policy is correct.

"If the revolutionary party," says Lenin, "has not a majority in the advanced detachments of the revolutionary classes and in the country, an uprising is out of the question" (see Vol. XXI, p. 282).

"Revolution is impossible without a change in the views of the majority of the working class, and this change is brought about by the political experience of the masses" (see Vol. XXV, p. 221).

"The proletarian vanguard has been won over ideologically. That is the main thing. Without this not even the first step towards victory can be made. But it is still a fairly long way from victory. Victory cannot be won with the vanguard alone. To throw the vanguard alone into the decisive battle, before the whole class, before the broad masses have taken up a position either of direct support of the vanguard, or at least of benevolent neutrality towards it, and one in which they cannot possibly support the enemy, would be not merely folly but a crime. And in order that actually the whole class, that actually the broad masses of the working people and those oppressed by capital may take up such a position, propaganda and agitation alone are not enough. For this the masses must have their own political experience" (*ibid.*, p. 228).

We know that this is precisely how our Party acted during the period from Lenin's April Theses to the October uprising of 1917. And it was precisely because it acted according to these directives of Lenin's that it was successful in the uprising.

Such, basically, are the conditions for correct mutual relations between the vanguard and the class. What does *leadership* mean when the policy of the Party is correct and the correct relations between the vanguard and the class are not upset?

Leadership under these circumstances means the ability to convince the masses of the correctness of the Party's policy; the ability to put forward and to carry out such slogans as bring the masses to the Party's positions and help them to realise through their own experience the correctness of the Party's policy; the ability to raise the masses to the Party's level of political consciousness, and thus secure the support of the masses and their readiness for the decisive struggle.

Therefore, the method of persuasion is the principal method of the Party's leadership of the working class.

"If we, in Russia today," says Lenin, "after two-and-a-half years of unprecedented victories over the bourgeoisie of Russia and the Entente, were to make 'recognition of the

45

dictatorship' a condition of trade-union membership, we should be committing a folly, we should be damaging our influence over the masses, we should be helping the Mensheviks. For the whole task of the Communists is to be able to *convince* the backward elements, to be able to work *among* them, and not to *fence themselves off* from them by artificial and childishly 'Left' slogans" (see Vol. XXV, p. 197).

This, of course, must not be understood in the sense that the Party must convince all the workers, down to the last man, and that only after this is it possible to proceed to action, that only after this is it possible to start operations. Not at all! It only means that before entering upon decisive political actions the Party must, by means of prolonged revolutionary work, secure for itself the support of the majority of the masses of the workers, or at least the benevolent neutrality of the majority of the class. Otherwise Lenin's thesis, that a necessary condition for victorious revolution is that the Party should win over the majority of the working class, would be devoid of all meaning.

Well, and what is to be done with the minority, if it does not wish, if it does not agree voluntarily to submit to the will of the majority? Can the Party, must the Party, enjoying the confidence of the majority, compel the minority to submit to the will of the majority? Yes, it can and it must. Leadership is ensured by the method of persuading the masses, as the principal method by which the Party influences the masses. This, however, does not preclude, but presupposes, the use of coercion, if such coercion is based on confidence in the Party and support for it on the part of the majority of the working class, if it is applied to the minority after the Party has convinced the majority.

It would be well to recall the controversies around this subject that took place in our Party during the discussion on the trade-union question. What was the mistake of the opposition, the mistake of the Tsektran,[14] at that time? Was it that the opposition then considered it possible to resort to coercion? No!

46

It, was not that. The mistake of the opposition at that time was that, being unable to convince the majority of the correctness of its position, having lost the confidence of the majority, it nevertheless began to apply coercion, began to insist on "shaking up" those who enjoyed the confidence of the majority.

Here is what Lenin said at that time, at the Tenth Congress of the Party, in his speech on the trade unions:

"In order to establish mutual relations and mutual confidence between the vanguard of the working class and the masses of the workers, it was necessary, if the Tsektran had made a mistake . . . to correct this mistake. But when people begin to defend this mistake, it becomes a source of political danger. Had not the utmost possible been done in the way of democracy in heeding the moods expressed here by Kutuzov, we would have met with political bankruptcy. *First we must convince, and then coerce. We must at all costs first convince, and then coerce.* We were not able to convince the broad masses, and we upset the correct relations between the vanguard and the masses" (see Vol. XXVI, p. 235).

Lenin says the same thing in his pamphlet *On the Trade Unions*[15]:

"We applied coercion correctly and successfully only when we were able to create beforehand a basis of conviction for it" (*ibid.*, p. 74).

And that is quite true, for without those conditions no leadership is possible. For only in that way can we ensure unity of action in the Party, if we are speaking of the Party, or unity of action of the class, if we are speaking of the class as a whole. Without this there is splitting, confusion and demoralisation in the ranks of the working class.

Such in general are the fundamentals of correct leadership of the working class by the Party.

Any other conception of leadership is syndicalism, anarchism, bureaucracy—anything you please, but not

Bolshevism, not Leninism.

The dictatorship of the proletariat cannot be counterposed to the leadership ("dictatorship") of the Party if correct mutual relations exist between the Party and the working class, between the vanguard and the masses of the workers. But from this it follows that it is all the more impermissible to identify the Party with the working class, the leadership ("dictatorship") of the Party with the dictatorship of the working class. *On the ground* that the "dictatorship" of the Party cannot be counterposed to the dictatorship of the proletariat, Sorin arrived at the wrong conclusion that *"the dictatorship of the proletariat is the dictatorship of our Party."*

But Lenin not only speaks of the impermissibility of such counterposition, he also speaks of the impermissibility of counterposing "the dictatorship of the masses to the dictatorship of the leaders." Would you, *on this ground*, have us identify the dictatorship of leaders with the dictatorship of the proletariat? If we took that line, we would have to say that *"the dictatorship of the proletariat is the dictatorship of our leaders."* But it is precisely to this absurdity that we are led, properly speaking, by the policy of identifying the "dictatorship" of the Party with the dictatorship of the proletariat. . . .

Where does Zinoviev stand on this subject?

In essence, Zinoviev shares Sorin's point of view of identifying the "dictatorship" of the Party with the dictatorship of the proletariat—with the difference, however, that Sorin expresses himself more openly and clearly, whereas Zinoviev "wriggles." One need only take, for instance, the following passage in Zinoviev's book *Leninism* to be convinced of this:

"What," says Zinoviev, "is the system existing in the U.S.S.R. from the standpoint of its class content? It is the dictatorship of the proletariat. What is the direct mainspring of power in the U.S.S.R.? Who exercises the power of the working class? The Communist Party! In this sense, *we have the*

48

dictatorship of the Party. What is the juridical form of power in the U.S.S.R.? What is the new type of state system that was created by the October Revolution? The Soviet system. The one does not in the least contradict the other."

That the one does not contradict the other is, of course, correct *if* by the dictatorship of the Party in relation to the working class as a whole we mean the leadership of the Party. But, how is it possible, *on this ground*, to place a sign of equality between the dictatorship of the proletariat and the "dictatorship" of the Party, between the Soviet system and the "dictatorship" of the Party? Lenin identified the system of Soviets with the dictatorship of the proletariat, and he was right, for the Soviets, *our* Soviets, are organisations which rally the labouring masses around the proletariat under the rally of the Party. But when, where, and in which of his writings did Lenin place a sign of equality between the "dictatorship" of the Party and the dictatorship of the proletariat, between the "dictatorship" of the Party and the system of Soviets, as Zinoviev does now? Neither the leadership ("dictatorship") of the Party nor the leadership ("dictatorship") of the leaders contradicts the dictatorship of the proletariat. Would you, *on this ground*, have us proclaim that our country is the country of the dictatorship of the proletariat, *that is to say*, the country of the dictatorship of the Party, *that is to say*, the country of the dictatorship of the leaders? And yet the "principle" of identifying the "dictatorship" of the Party with the dictatorship of the proletariat, which Zinoviev enunciates surreptitiously and uncourageously, leads precisely to this absurdity.

In Lenin's numerous works I have been able to note only five cases in which he touches, in passing, on the question of the dictatorship of the Party.

The first case is in his controversy with the Socialist-Revolutionaries and the Mensheviks, where he says:

"When we are reproached with the dictatorship of one party, and when, as you have heard, a proposal is made to establish a united socialist front, we reply: 'Yes, the dictatorship of one party! We stand by it, and cannot depart from it, for it is that Party which, in the course of decades, has won the position of vanguard of the whole factory and industrial proletariat'" (see Vol. XXIV, p. 423).

The second case is in his "Letter to the Workers and Peasants in Connection with the Victory over Kolchak," in which he says:

"Some people (especially the Mensheviks and the Socialist Revolutionaries—all of them, even the 'Lefts' among them) are trying to scare the peasants with the bogey of the 'dictatorship of one party,' the Party of Bolsheviks, Communists.

"The peasants have learned from the instance of Kolchak not to be afraid of this bogey.

"Either the dictatorship (i.e., iron rule) of the landlords and capitalists, or the dictatorship of the working class" (see Vol. XXIV, p. 436).

The third case is Lenin's speech at the Second Congress of the Comintern in his controversy with Tanner. I have quoted it above.

The fourth case is a few lines in the pamphlet *"Left-Wing" Communism, an Infantile Disorder*. The passages in question have already been quoted above.

And the fifth case is in his draft outline of the dictatorship of the proletariat, published in the *Lenin Miscellany*, Volume III, where there is a sub-heading "Dictatorship of One Party" (see *Lenin Miscellany*, Vol. III, p. 497).

It should be noted that in two out of the five cases, the last and the second, Lenin puts the words "dictatorship of one party" in quotation marks, thus clearly emphasising the inexact, figurative sense of this formula.

It should also be noted that in every one of these cases, by the "dictatorship of the Party" Lenin meant dictatorship ("iron rule") over the "landlords and capitalists," and not over the working class, contrary to the slanderous fabrications of Kautsky and Co.

It is characteristic that in *none* of his works, major or secondary, in which Lenin discusses or merely alludes to the dictatorship of the proletariat and the role of the Party in the system of the dictatorship of the proletariat, is there any hint whatever that "the dictatorship of the proletariat is the dictatorship of our Party." On the contrary, every page, every line of these works cries out against such a formula (see *The State and Revolution, The Proletarian Revolution and the Renegade Kautsky, "Left-Wing" Communism, an Infantile Disorder,* etc.).

Even more characteristic is the fact that in the theses of the Second Congress of the Comintern[16] on the role of a political party, which were drawn up under the direct guidance of Lenin, and to which Lenin repeatedly referred in his speeches as a model of the correct formulation of the role and tasks of the Party, we find *not one word,* literally *not one word,* about dictatorship of the Party.

What does all this indicate?

It indicates that:

a) Lenin did not regard the formula "dictatorship of the Party" as irreproachable and exact, for which reason it is very rarely used in Lenin's works, and is sometimes put in quotation marks;

b) on the few occasions that Lenin was obliged, in controversy with opponents, to speak of the dictatorship of the Party, he usually referred to the "dictatorship of *one* party," i.e., to the fact that our Party holds power *alone,* that it *does not share* power with other parties. Moreover, he always made it clear that the dictatorship of the Party *in relation to the working class* meant the leadership of the Party, its leading role;

c) in all those cases in which Lenin thought it necessary to give a scientific definition of the role of the Party in the system of the dictatorship of the proletariat, he spoke *exclusively* of the leading role of the Party in relation to the working class (and there are thousands of such cases);

d) that is why it never "occurred" to Lenin to include the formula "dictatorship of the Party" in the fundamental resolution on the role of the Party—I have in mind the resolution adopted at the Second Congress of the Comintern;

e) the comrades who identify, or try to identify, the "dictatorship" of the Party and, therefore, the "dictatorship of the leaders" with the dictatorship of the proletariat are wrong from the point of view of Leninism, and are politically short-sighted, for they thereby violate the conditions for correct mutual relations between the vanguard and the class.

This is apart from the fact that the formula "dictatorship of the Party," when taken without the above-mentioned reservations, can give rise to quite a number of dangers and political set-backs in our practical work. This formula, taken without reservations, says, as it were:

a) *to the non-Party masses*: don't dare to contradict, don't dare to argue, for the Party can do everything, for we have the dictatorship of the Party;

b) *to the Party cadres*: act more boldly, tighten the screw, there is no need to heed what the non-Party masses say, we have the dictatorship of the Party;

c) *to the top leadership of the Party*: you may indulge in the luxury of a certain amount of complacency, you may even become conceited, for we have the dictatorship of the Party, and, "consequently," the dictatorship of the leaders.

It is opportune to call attention to these dangers precisely at the present moment, in a period when the political activity of the masses is rising, when the readiness of the Party to heed the voice of the masses is of particular value to us, when attention to the requirements of the masses is a fundamental precept of our Party, when it is incumbent upon the Party to display particular caution and particular flexibility in its policy, when the danger of becoming conceited is one of the most serious dangers confronting the Party in its task of correctly leading the masses.

One cannot but recall Lenin's golden words at the Eleventh Congress of our Party:

"Among the mass of the people we (the Communists— *J. St.*) are after all but a drop in the ocean, and we can administer only when we properly express what the people are conscious of. Unless we do this the Communist Party will not lead the proletariat, the proletariat will not lead the masses, and the whole machine will collapse" (see Vol. XXVII, p. 256).

"Properly express what the people are conscious of"— this is precisely the necessary condition that ensures for the Party the honourable role of the principal guiding force in the system of the dictatorship of the proletariat.

VI. The Question of the Victory of Socialism in One Country

The pamphlet *The Foundations of Leninism* (May 1924, first edition) contains two formulations on the question of the victory of socialism in one country. The first of these says:

"Formerly, the victory of the revolution in one country was considered impossible, on the assumption that it would require the combined action of the proletarians of all or at least of a majority of the advanced countries to achieve victory over the bourgeoisie. Now this point of view no longer fits in with the facts. Now we must proceed from the possibility of such a victory, for the uneven and spasmodic character of the development of the various capitalist countries under the conditions of imperialism, the development within imperialism of catastrophic contradictions leading to inevitable wars, the growth of the revolutionary movement in all countries of the world—all this leads, not only to the possibility, but also to the necessity of the victory of the proletariat in individual countries" (see *The Foundations of Leninism*[17]).

This thesis is quite correct and needs no comment. It is directed against the theory of the Social-Democrats, who regard the seizure of power by the proletariat in one country, without the simultaneous victory of the revolution in other countries, as utopian.

But the pamphlet *The Foundations of Leninism* contains a second formulation, which says:

"But the overthrow of the power of the bourgeoisie and establishment of the power of the proletariat in one country does not yet mean that the complete victory of socialism has been ensured. The principal task of socialism—the organisation of socialist production—has still to be fulfilled. Can this task be fulfilled, can the final victory of socialism be achieved in one country, without the joint efforts of the proletarians in several advanced countries? No, it cannot. To overthrow the bourgeoisie the efforts of one country are sufficient; this is proved by the history of our revolution. For the final victory of socialism, for the organisation of socialist production, the efforts of one country, particularly of a peasant country like Russia, are insufficient; for that, the efforts of the proletarians of several advanced countries are required" (see *The Foundations of Leninism*, first edition[18]).

This second formulation was directed against the assertions of the critics of Leninism, against the Trotskyists, who declared that the dictatorship of the proletariat in one country, in the absence of victory in other countries, could not "hold out in the face of a conservative Europe."

To that extent—but only to that extent—this formulation was then (May 1924) adequate, and undoubtedly it was of some service.

Subsequently, however, when the criticism of Leninism in this sphere had already been overcome in the Party, when a new question had come to the fore—the question of the possibility of building a complete socialist society by the efforts of our country, without help from abroad—the second formulation became obviously inadequate, and therefore incorrect.

What is the defect in this formulation?

Its defect is that it joins two different questions into one: it joins the question of the *possibility* of building socialism by the efforts of one country—which must be answered in the affirmative—with the question whether a country in which the dictatorship of the proletariat exists can consider itself *fully guaranteed* against intervention, and consequently against the restoration of the old order, without a victorious revolution in a number of other countries—which must be answered in the negative. This is apart from the fact that this formulation may give occasion for thinking that the organisation of a socialist society by the efforts of one country is impossible—which, of course, is incorrect.

On this ground I modified and corrected this formulation in my pamphlet *The October Revolution and the Tactics of the Russian Communists* (December 1924); I divided the question into two—into the question of a *full guarantee against the restoration of the bourgeois order*, and the question of the *possibility of building a complete socialist society* in one country. This was effected, in the first place, by treating the "complete victory of socialism" as a "full guarantee against the restoration of the old order," which is possible only through "the joint efforts of the proletarians of several countries"; and, secondly, by proclaiming, on the basis of Lenin's pamphlet *On Co-operation*,[19] the indisputable truth that we have all that is necessary for building a complete socialist society (see *The October Revolution and the Tactics of the Russian Communists*).

It was this new formulation of the question that formed the basis for the well-known resolution of the Fourteenth Party Conference "The Tasks of the Comintern and the R.C.P.(B.),"[20] which examines the question of the victory of socialism in one country in connection with the stabilisation of capitalism (April 1925), and considers that the building of socialism by the efforts of our country is possible and necessary.

This new formulation also served as the basis for my pamphlet *The Results of the Work of the Fourteenth Conference of the R.C.P.(B.)* published in May 1925, immediately after the Fourteenth Party Conference.

With regard to the presentation of the question of the victory of socialism in one country, this pamphlet states:

"Our country exhibits two groups of contradictions. One group consists of the internal contradictions that exist between the proletariat and the peasantry (this refers to the building of socialism in one country—*J. St.*). The other group consists of the external contradictions that exist between our country, as the land of socialism, and all the other countries, as lands of capitalism (this refers to the final victory of socialism—*J. St.*)." . . . "Anyone who confuses the first group of contradictions, which can be overcome entirely by the efforts of one country, with the second group of contradictions, the solution of which requires the efforts of the proletarians of several countries, commits a gross error against Leninism. He is either a muddle-head or an incorrigible opportunist" (see *The Results of the Work of the Fourteenth Conference of the R.C.P. (B.)*.[21])

On the question of the victory of socialism in our country, the pamphlet states:

"We can build socialism, and we will build it together with the peasantry under the leadership of the working class". . . for "under the dictatorship of the proletariat we possess . . . all that is needed to build a complete socialist society, overcoming all internal difficulties, for we can and must overcome them by our own efforts" (*ibid.*[22]).

On the question of the *final* victory of socialism, it states:

"The final victory of socialism is the full guarantee against attempts at intervention, and hence against restoration, for any serious attempt at restoration can take place only with serious support from outside, only with the support of international capital. Therefore, the support of our revolution by the workers of all countries, and still more the victory of the workers in at least several countries, is a necessary condition for fully guaranteeing the first victorious country against attempts at intervention and restoration, a necessary condition for the final victory of socialism" (*ibid.*[23]).

Clear, one would think.

It is well known that this question was treated in the

same spirit in my pamphlet *Questions and Answers* (June 1925) and in the political report of the Central Committee to the Fourteenth Congress of the C.P.S.U.(B.)[24] (December 1925).

Such are the facts.

These facts, I think, are known to all the comrades, including Zinoviev.

If now, nearly two years after the ideological struggle in the Party and after the resolution that was adopted at the Fourteenth Party Conference (April 1925), Zinoviev finds it possible in his reply to the discussion at the Fourteenth Party Congress (December 1925) to dig up the old and quite inadequate formula contained in Stalin's pamphlet written in April 1924, and to make it the basis for deciding the already decided question of the victory of socialism in one country— then this peculiar trick of his only goes to show that he has got completely muddled on this question. To drag the Party back after it has moved forward, to evade the resolution of the Fourteenth Party Conference after it has been confirmed by a Plenum of the Central Committee,[25] means to become hopelessly entangled in contradictions, to have no faith in the cause of building socialism, to abandon the path of Lenin, and to acknowledge one's own defeat.

What is meant by the *possibility* of the victory of socialism in one country?

It means the possibility of solving the contradictions between the proletariat and the peasantry by means of the internal forces of our country, the possibility of the proletariat seizing power and using that power to build a complete socialist society in our country, with the sympathy and the support of the proletarians of other countries, but without the preliminary victory of the proletarian revolution in other countries.

Without, such a possibility, building socialism is building without prospects, building without being sure that socialism will be completely built. It is no use engaging in building socialism without being sure that we can build it completely, without being sure that the technical backwardness of our country is not an insuperable obstacle to the building of a complete socialist society. To deny such a possibility means disbelief in the cause of building socialism, departure from Leninism.

What is meant by the *impossibility* of the complete, final victory of socialism in one country without the victory of the revolution in other countries?

It means the impossibility of having a full guarantee against intervention, and consequently against the restoration of the bourgeois order, without the victory of the revolution in at least a number of countries. To deny this indisputable thesis means departure from internationalism, departure from Leninism.

"We are living," says Lenin, "not merely in a state, but *in a system of states*, and the existence of the Soviet Republic side by side with imperialist states for a long time is unthinkable. One or the other must triumph in the end. And before that end comes, a series of frightful collisions between the Soviet Republic and the bourgeois states will be inevitable. That means that if the ruling class, the proletariat, wants to, and will hold sway, it must prove this by its military organisation also" (see Vol. XXIV, p. 122).

"We have before us," says Lenin in another passage, "a certain equilibrium, which is in the highest degree unstable, but an unquestionable, an indisputable equilibrium nevertheless. Will it last long? I do not know and, I think, it is impossible to know. And therefore we must exercise very great caution. And the first precept of our policy, the first lesson to be learned from our governmental activities during the past year, the lesson which all the workers and peasants must learn, is that we must be on the alert, we must remember that we are surrounded by people, classes and governments who openly express their intense hatred for us. We must remember that we are at all times but a hair's breadth from every manner of invasion" (see Vol. XXVII, p. 117).

Clear, one would think.

Where does Zinoviev stand as regards the question of the victory of socialism in one country?

Listen:

"By the final victory of socialism is meant, at least: 1) the abolition of classes, and therefore 2) the abolition of the dictatorship of one class, in this case the dictatorship of the proletariat." . . . "In order to get a clearer idea of how the question stands here, in the U.S.S.R., in the year 1925," says Zinoviev further, "we must distinguish between two things: 1) the assured *possibility* of engaging in building socialism—such a possibility, it stands to reason, is quite conceivable within the limits of one country; and 2) the final construction and consolidation of socialism, i.e., the achievement of a socialist system, of a socialist society."

What can all this signify?

It signifies that by the final victory of socialism in one country Zinoviev understands, not a guarantee against intervention and restoration, but the possibility of completely building socialist society. And by the victory of socialism in one country Zinoviev understands the kind of building socialism which cannot and should not lead to completely building socialism. Building at haphazard, without prospects, building socialism although completely building a socialist society is impossible—such is Zinoviev's position.

To engage in building socialism *without the possibility* of completely building it, *knowing that it cannot be completely built*—such are the absurdities in which Zinoviev has involved himself.

But this is a mockery of the question, not a solution of it!

60

Here is another extract from Zinoviev's reply to the discussion at the Fourteenth Party Congress:

"Take a look, for instance, at what Comrade Yakovlev went so far as to say at the last Kursk Gubernia Party Conference. He asks: 'Is it possible for us, surrounded as we are on all sides by capitalist enemies, to completely build socialism in one country under such conditions?' And he answers: 'On the basis of all that has been said we have the right to say not only that we are building socialism, but that in spite of the fact that for the time being we are alone, that for the time being we are the only Soviet country, the only Soviet state in the world, we shall completely build socialism' (*Kurskaya Pravda*, No. 279, December 8, 1925). *Is this the Leninist method of presenting the question*," Zinoviev asks, "*does not this smack of national narrow-mindedness?*"

Thus, according to Zinoviev, to recognise the possibility of completely building socialism in one country means adopting the point of view of national narrow-mindedness, while to deny such a possibility means adopting the point of view of internationalism.

But if that is true, is it at all worth while fighting for victory over the capitalist elements in our economy?

Does it not follow from this that such a victory is impossible?

Capitulation to the capitalist elements in our economy— that is what the inherent logic of Zinoviev's line of argument leads us to.

And this absurdity, which has nothing in common with Leninism, is presented to us by Zinoviev as "internationalism," as "100 per cent Leninism"!

I assert that on this most important question of building socialism Zinoviev is deserting Leninism and slipping to the standpoint of the Menshevik Sukhanov.

Let us turn to Lenin. Here is what he said about the victory of socialism in one country even before the October Revolution, in August 1915:

"Uneven economic and political development is an absolute law of capitalism. Hence, the victory of socialism is possible first in several or even in one capitalist country taken separately. The victorious proletariat of that country, having expropriated the capitalists and *organised socialist production*, would stand up against the rest of the world, the capitalist world, attracting to its cause the oppressed classes of other countries, raising revolts in those countries against the capitalists, and in the event of necessity coming out even with armed force against the exploiting classes and their states" (see Vol. XVIII, pp. 232-33).

What is meant by Lenin's phrase "having . . . organised socialist production" which I have stressed? It means that the proletariat of the victorious country, having seized power, *can* and *must* organise socialist production. And what does to "organise socialist production" mean? It means completely building a socialist society. It scarcely needs proof that this clear and definite statement of Lenin's requires no further comment. Otherwise Lenin's call for the seizure of power by the proletariat in October 1917 would be incomprehensible.

You see that this clear thesis of Lenin's, in comparison with Zinoviev's muddled and anti-Leninist "thesis" that we can engage in building socialism "within the limits of one country," although it is *impossible* to build it completely, is as different from the latter as the heavens from the earth.

The statement quoted above was made by Lenin in 1915, before the proletariat had taken power. But perhaps he modified his views after the experience of taking power, after 1917? Let us turn to Lenin's pamphlet *On Co-operation*, written in 1923.

"As a matter of fact;" says Lenin, "state power over all

large-scale means of production, state power in the hands of the proletariat, the alliance of this proletariat with the many millions of small and very small peasants, the assured leadership of the peasantry by the proletariat, etc.—is not this all that is necessary for building a complete socialist society from the co-operatives, from the co-operatives alone, which we formerly looked down upon as huckstering and which from a certain aspect we have the right to look down upon as such now, under NEP? *Is this not all that is necessary for building a complete socialist society?* This is not yet the building of socialist society, but *it is all that is necessary and sufficient for this building*" (see Vol. XXVII, p. 392).

In other words, we can and must build a complete socialist society, for we have at our disposal all that is necessary and sufficient for this building.

I think it would be difficult to express oneself more clearly.

Compare this classical thesis of Lenin's with the anti-Leninist rebuke Zinoviev administered to Yakovlev, and you will realise that Yakovlev was only repeating Lenin's words about the possibility of completely building socialism in one country, whereas Zinoviev, by attacking this thesis and castigating Yakovlev, deserted Lenin and adopted the point of view of the Menshevik Sukhanov, the point of view that it is impossible to build socialism completely in our country owing to its technical backwardness.

One can only wonder why we took power in October 1917 if we did not count on completely building socialism.

We should not have taken power in October 1917—this is the conclusion to which the inherent logic of Zinoviev's line of argument leads us.

I assert further that in the highly important question of the victory of socialism Zinoviev has gone counter to the definite decisions of our Party, as registered in the well-known

63

resolution of the Fourteenth Party Conference "The Tasks of the Comintern and the R.C.P.(B.) in Connection with the Enlarged Plenum of the E.C.C.I."

Let us turn to this resolution. Here is what it says about the victory of socialism in one country:

"The existence of two directly opposite social systems gives rise to the constant menace of capitalist blockade, of other forms of economic pressure, of armed intervention, of restoration. Consequently, the only guarantee of the *final victory of socialism*, i.e., *the guarantee against restoration*, is a victorious socialist revolution in a number of countries. . . ." "Leninism teaches that the *final* victory of socialism, *in the sense of a full guarantee against the restoration* of bourgeois relationships, is possible only on an international scale. . . . " "But it *does not follow* from this that it is impossible to build a *complete socialist society* in a backward country like Russia, without the 'state aid' (Trotsky) of countries more developed technically and economically" (see the resolution[26]).

As you see, the resolution interprets the final victory of socialism as a guarantee against intervention and restoration, *in complete contrast* to Zinoviev's interpretation in his book *Leninism.*

As you see, the resolution recognises the possibility of building a complete socialist society in a backward country like Russia without the "state aid" of countries more developed technically and economically, *in complete contrast* to what Zinoviev said when he rebuked Yakovlev in his reply to the discussion at the Fourteenth Party Congress.

How else can this be described if not as a struggle on Zinoviev's part *against* the resolution of the Fourteenth Party Conference?

Of course, Party resolutions are sometimes not free from error. Sometimes they contain mistakes. Speaking generally, one may assume that the resolution of the Fourteenth Party

Conference also contains certain errors. Perhaps Zinoviev thinks that this resolution is erroneous. But then he should say so clearly and openly, as befits a Bolshevik. For some reason or other, however, Zinoviev does not do so. He preferred to choose another path, that of attacking the resolution of the Fourteenth Party Conference from the rear, while keeping silent about this resolution and refraining from any open criticism of the resolution. Zinoviev evidently thinks that this will be the best way of achieving his purpose. And he has but one purpose, namely—to "improve" the resolution, and to amend Lenin "just a little bit." It scarcely needs proof that Zinoviev has made a mistake in his calculations.

What is Zinoviev's mistake due to? What is the root of this mistake?

The root of this mistake, in my opinion, lies in Zinoviev's conviction that the technical backwardness of our country is an *insuperable* obstacle to the building of a complete socialist society; that the proletariat cannot completely build socialism owing to the technical backwardness of our country. Zinoviev and Kamenev once tried to raise this argument at a meeting of the Central Committee of the Party prior to the April Party Conference.[27] But they received a rebuff and were compelled to retreat, and *formally* they submitted to the opposite point of view, the point of view of the majority of the Central Committee. But although he formally submitted to it, Zinoviev has continued to wage a struggle against it all the time. Here is what the Moscow Committee of our Party says about this "incident" in the Central Committee of the R.C.P:(B.) in its "Reply" to the letter of the Leningrad Gubernia Party Conference[28]:

"Recently, in the Political Bureau, Kamenev and Zinoviev advocated the point of view that we cannot cope with the internal difficulties due to our technical and economic backwardness unless an international revolution comes to our rescue. We, however, with the majority of the members of the

65

Central Committee, think that we can build socialism, are building it, and will completely build it, notwithstanding our technical backwardness and in spite of it. We think that the work of building will proceed far more slowly, of course, than in the conditions of a world victory; nevertheless, we are making progress and will continue to do so. We also believe that the view held by Kamenev and Zinoviev expresses disbelief in the internal forces of our working class and of the peasant masses who follow its lead. We believe that it is a departure from the Leninist position" (see "Reply").

This document appeared in the press during the first sittings of the Fourteenth Party Congress. Zinoviev, of course, had the opportunity of attacking this document at the congress. It is characteristic that Zinoviev and Kamenev found no arguments against this grave accusation directed against them by the Moscow Committee of our Party. Was this accidental? I think not. The accusation, apparently, hit the mark. Zinoviev and Kamenev "replied" to this accusation by silence, because they had no "card to beat it."

The "New Opposition" is offended because Zinoviev is accused of disbelief in the victory of socialist construction in our country. But if after a whole year of discussion on the question of the victory of socialism in one country; after Zinoviev's view-point has been rejected by the Political Bureau of the Central Committee (April 1925); after the Party has arrived at a definite opinion on this question, recorded in the well-known resolution of the Fourteenth Party Conference (April 1925)—if, after all this, Zinoviev ventures to oppose the point of view of the Party in his book *Leninism* (September 1925), if he then repeats this opposition at the Fourteenth Party Congress—how can all this, this stubbornness, this persistence in his error, be explained if not by the fact that Zinoviev is infected, hopelessly infected, with disbelief in the victory of socialist construction in our country?

It pleases Zinoviev to regard this disbelief of his as

internationalism. But since when have we come to regard departure from Leninism on a cardinal question of Leninism as internationalism?

Will it not be more correct to say that it is not the Party but Zinoviev who is sinning against internationalism and the international revolution? For what is our country, the country "that is building socialism," if not the base of the world revolution? But can it be a real base of the world revolution if it is incapable of completely building a socialist society? Can it remain the mighty centre of attraction for the workers of all countries that it undoubtedly is now, if it is incapable of achieving victory at home over the capitalist elements in our economy, the victory of socialist construction? I think not. But does it not follow from this that disbelief in the victory of socialist construction, the dissemination of such disbelief, will lead to our country being discredited as the base of the world revolution? And if our country is discredited the world revolutionary movement will be weakened. How did Messrs. the Social-Democrats try to scare the workers away from us? By preaching that "the Russians will not get anywhere." What are we beating the Social-Democrats with now, when we are attracting a whole series of workers' delegations to our country and thereby strengthening the position of communism all over the world? By our successes in building socialism. Is it not obvious, then, that whoever disseminates disbelief in our successes in building socialism thereby indirectly helps the Social-Democrats, reduces the sweep of the international revolutionary movement, and inevitably departs from internationalism? . . .

You see that Zinoviev is in no better position in regard to his "internationalism" than in regard to his "100 per cent Leninism" on the question of building socialism in one country.

That is why the Fourteenth Party Congress rightly defined the views of the "New Opposition" as "disbelief in the cause of socialist construction," as "a distortion of Leninism."[29]

VII. The Fight for the Victory of Socialism Construction

I think that disbelief in the victory of socialist construction is the principal error of the "New Opposition." In my opinion, it is the principal error because from it spring all the other errors of the "New Opposition." The errors of the "New Opposition" on the questions of NEP, state capitalism, the nature of our socialist industry, the role of the co-operatives under the dictatorship of the proletariat, the methods of fighting the kulaks, the role and importance of the middle peasantry—all these errors are to be traced to the principal error of the opposition, to disbelief in the possibility of completely building a socialist society by the efforts of our country.

What is disbelief in the victory of socialist construction in our country?

It is, first of all, lack of confidence that, owing to certain conditions of development in our country, the main mass of the peasantry *can be drawn* into the work of socialist construction.

It is, secondly, lack of confidence that the proletariat of our country, which holds the key positions in our national economy, *is capable* of drawing the main mass of the peasantry into the work of socialist construction. It is from these theses that the opposition tacitly proceeds in its arguments about the paths of our development—no matter whether it does so consciously or unconsciously.

Can the main mass of the Soviet peasantry be drawn into the work of socialist construction?

In the pamphlet *The Foundations of Leninism* there are two main theses on this subject:

1) "The peasantry in the Soviet Union must not be confused with the peasantry in the West. A peasantry that has

been schooled in three revolutions, that fought against the tsar and the power of the bourgeoisie side by side with the proletariat and under the leadership of the proletariat, a peasantry that has received land and peace at the hands of the proletarian revolution and by reason of this has become the reserve of the proletariat—such a peasantry cannot but be different from a peasantry which during the bourgeois revolution fought under the leadership of the liberal bourgeoisie, which received land at the hands of that bourgeoisie, and in view of this became the reserve of the bourgeoisie. It scarcely needs proof that the Soviet peasantry, which has learnt to appreciate its political friendship and *political* collaboration with the proletariat and which owes its freedom to this friendship and collaboration, cannot but represent exceptionally favourable material for *economic* collaboration with the proletariat."

2) "Agriculture in Russia must not be confused with agriculture in the West. There, agriculture is developing along the ordinary lines of capitalism, under conditions of profound differentiation among the peasantry, with large landed estates and private capitalist latifundia at one extreme and pauperism, destitution and wage slavery at the other. Owing to this, disintegration and decay are quite natural there. Not so in Russia. Here agriculture cannot develop along such a path, if for no other reason than that the existence of Soviet power and the nationalisation of the principal instruments and means of production preclude such a development. In Russia the development of agriculture must proceed along a different path, along the path of organising millions of small and middle peasants in co-operatives, along the path of developing in the countryside a mass co-operative movement supported by the state by means of preferential credits. Lenin rightly pointed out in his articles on co-operation that the development of agriculture in our country must proceed along a new path, along the path of drawing the majority of the peasants into socialist construction through the co-operatives, along the path of

gradually introducing into agriculture the principles of collectivism, first in the sphere of marketing and later in the sphere of production of agricultural products. . . .

"It scarcely needs proof that the vast majority of the peasantry will eagerly take this new path of development, rejecting the path of private capitalist latifundia and wage slavery, the path of destitution and ruin."[30]

Are these theses correct?

I think that both theses are correct and incontrovertible for the whole of our construction period under the conditions of NEP.

They are merely the expression of Lenin's well-known theses on the bond between the proletariat and the peasantry, on the inclusion of the peasant farms in the system of socialist development of our country; of his theses that the proletariat must march towards socialism together with the main mass of the peasantry, that the organisation of the vast masses of the peasantry in co-operatives is the high road of socialist construction in the countryside, that with the growth of our socialist industry, "for us, the more growth of co-operation is identical . . . with the growth of socialism" (see Vol. XXVII, p. 396).

Indeed, along what path can and must the development of peasant economy in our country proceed? Peasant economy is not capitalist economy. Peasant economy, if you take the overwhelming majority of the peasant farms, is small commodity economy. And what is peasant small commodity economy? It is economy standing at the cross-roads between capitalism and socialism. It may develop in the direction of capitalism, as it is now doing in capitalist countries, or in the direction of socialism, as it must do here, in our country, under the dictatorship of the proletariat.

Whence this instability, this lack of independence of peasant economy? How is it to be explained?

It is to be explained by the scattered character of the peasant farms, their lack of organisation, their dependence on the towns, on industry, on the credit system, on the character of the state power in the country, and, lastly, by the well-known fact that the countryside follows, and necessarily must follow, the town both in material and in cultural matters.

The capitalist path of development of peasant economy means development through profound differentiation among the peasantry, with large latifundia at one extreme and mass impoverishment at the other. Such a path of development is inevitable in capitalist countries, because the countryside, peasant economy, is dependent on the towns, on industry, on credit concentrated in the towns, on the character of the state power—and in the towns it is the bourgeoisie, capitalist industry, the capitalist credit system and the capitalist state power that hold sway.

Is this path of development of peasant farms obligatory for our country, where the towns have quite a different aspect, where industry is in the hands of the proletariat, where transport, the credit system, the state power, etc., are concentrated in the hands of the proletariat, where the nationalisation of the land is a universal law of the country? Of course not. On the contrary. Precisely because the towns do lead the countryside, while we have in the towns the rule of the proletariat, which holds all the key positions of national economy—precisely for this reason the peasant farms in their development must proceed along a different path, the path of socialist construction.

What is this path?

It is the path of the mass organisation of millions of peasant farms into co-operatives in all spheres of co-operation, the path of uniting the scattered peasant farms around socialist industry, the path of implanting the elements of collectivism among the peasantry at first in the sphere of *marketing* agricultural produce and supplying the peasant farms with the

71

products of urban industry and later in the sphere of agricultural *production*.

And the further we advance the more this path becomes inevitable under the conditions of the dictatorship of the proletariat, because co-operative marketing, co-operative supplying, and, finally, co-operative credit and production (agricultural co-operatives) are the only way to promote the welfare of the countryside, the only way to save the broad masses of the peasantry from poverty and ruin.

It is said that our peasantry, by its position, is not socialist, and, therefore, incapable of socialist development. It is true, of course, that the peasantry, by its position, is not socialist. But this is no argument against the development of the peasant farms along the path of socialism, once it has been proved that the countryside follows the town, and in the towns it is socialist industry that holds sway. The peasantry, by its position, was not socialist at the time of the October Revolution either, and it did not by any means want to establish socialism in our country. At that time it strove mainly for the abolition of the power of the landlords and for the ending of the war, for the establishment of peace. Nevertheless, it followed the lead of the socialist proletariat. Why? Because the overthrow of the bourgeoisie and the seizure of power by the socialist proletariat was at that time the only way of getting out of the imperialist war, the only way of establishing peace. Because there was no other way at that time, nor could there be any. Because our Party was able to hit upon that degree of the combination of the specific interests of the peasantry (the overthrow of the landlords, peace) with, and their subordination to, the general interests of the country (the dictatorship of the proletariat) which proved acceptable and advantageous to the peasantry. And so the peasantry, in spite of its non-socialist character, at that time followed the lead of the socialist proletariat.

The same must be said about socialist construction in our country, about drawing the peasantry into the channel of this construction. The peasantry is non-socialist by its position. But it must, and certainly will, take the path of socialist development, for there is not, and cannot be, any other way of saving the peasantry from poverty and ruin except the bond with the proletariat, except the bond with socialist industry, except the inclusion of peasant economy in the common channel of socialist development by the mass organisation of the peasantry in co-operatives.

But why precisely by the mass organisation of the peasantry in co-operatives?

Because in the mass organisation in co-operatives "we have found that degree of the combination of private interest, private trading interest, with state supervision and control of this interest, that degree of its subordination to the general interests" (*Lenin*)[31] which is acceptable and advantageous to the peasantry and which ensures the proletariat the possibility of drawing the main mass of the peasantry into the work of socialist construction. It is precisely because it is advantageous to the peasantry to organise the sale of its products and the purchase of machines for its farms through co-operatives, it is precisely for that reason that it should and will proceed along the path of mass organisation in co-operatives.

What does the mass organisation of peasant farms in co-operatives mean when we have the supremacy of socialist industry?

It means that peasant small commodity economy *abandons* the old capitalist path, which is fraught with mass ruin for the peasantry, and *goes over* to the new path of development, the path of socialist construction.

This is why the fight for the new path of development of peasant economy, the fight to draw the main mass of the peasantry into the work of socialist construction, is the immediate task facing our Party.

The Fourteenth Congress of the C.P.S.U.(B.), therefore,

was right in declaring:

"The main path of building socialism in the countryside consists in using the growing economic leadership of socialist state industry, of the state credit institutions, and of the other key positions in the hands of the proletariat to draw the main mass of the peasantry into co-operative organisation and to ensure for this organisation a socialist development, while utilising, overcoming and ousting its capitalist elements" (see Resolution of the Congress on the Report of the Central Committee[32]).

The profound mistake of the "New Opposition" lies in the fact that it does not believe in this new path of development of the peasantry, that it does not see, or does not understand, the absolute inevitability of this path under the conditions of the dictatorship of the proletariat. And it does not understand this because it does not believe in the victory of socialist construction in our country, it does not believe in the capacity of our proletariat to lead the peasantry along the path to socialism.

Hence the failure to understand the dual character of NEP, the exaggeration of the negative aspects of NEP and the treatment of NEP as being mainly a retreat.

Hence the exaggeration of the role of the capitalist elements in our economy, and the belittling of the role of the levers of our socialist development (socialist industry, the credit system, the co-operatives, the rule of the proletariat, etc.).

Hence the failure to understand the socialist nature of our state industry, and the doubts concerning the correctness of Lenin's co-operative plan.

Hence the inflated accounts of differentiation in the countryside, the panic in face of the kulak, the belittling of the role of the middle peasant, the attempts to thwart the Party's policy of securing a firm alliance with the middle peasant, and, in general, the wobbling from one side to another on the question of the Party's policy in the countryside.

Hence the failure to understand the tremendous work of the Party in drawing the vast masses of the workers and peasants into building up industry and agriculture, revitalising the co-operatives and the Soviets, administering the country, combating bureaucracy, improving and remodelling our state apparatus—work which marks a new stage of development and without which no socialist construction is conceivable.

Hence the hopelessness and consternation in face of the difficulties of our work of construction, the doubts about the possibility of industrialising our country, the pessimistic chatter about degeneration of the Party, etc.

Over there, among the bourgeoisie, all is going on fairly well, but here, among the proletarians, things are fairly bad; unless the revolution in the West takes place pretty soon, our cause is lost—such is the general tone of the "New Opposition" which, in my opinion, is a liquidationist tone, but which, for some reason or other (probably in jest), the opposition tries to pass off as "internationalism."

NEP is capitalism, says the opposition. NEP is mainly a retreat, says Zinoviev. All this, of course, is untrue. In actual fact, NEP is the Party's policy, permitting a struggle between the socialist and the capitalist elements and aimed at the victory of the socialist elements over the capitalist elements. In actual fact, NEP only began as a retreat, but it aimed at regrouping our forces during the retreat and launching an offensive. In actual fact, we have been on the offensive for several years now, and are attacking successfully, developing our industry, developing Soviet trade, and ousting private capital.

But what is the meaning of the thesis that NEP is capitalism, that NEP is mainly a retreat? What does this thesis proceed from?

It proceeds from the wrong assumption that what is now taking place in our country is simply the restoration of capitalism, simply a "return" to capitalism. This assumption alone can explain the doubts of the opposition regarding the socialist nature of our industry. This assumption alone can explain the panic of the opposition in face of the kulak. This assumption alone can explain the haste with which the opposition seized upon the inaccurate statistics on differentiation in the peasantry. This assumption alone can explain the opposition's special forgetfulness of the fact that the middle peasant is the central figure in our agriculture. This assumption alone can explain the under-estimation of the importance of the middle peasant and the doubts concerning Lenin's cooperative plan. This assumption alone can serve to "substantiate" the "New Opposition's" disbelief in the new path of development of the countryside, the path of drawing it into the work of socialist construction.

As a matter of fact, what is taking place in our country now is not a one-sided process of restoration of capitalism, but a double process of development of capitalism and development of socialism—a contradictory process of struggle between the socialist and the capitalist elements, a process in which the socialist elements are overcoming the capitalist elements. This is equally incontestable as regards the towns, where state industry is the basis of socialism, and as regards the countryside, here the main foothold for socialist development is mass co-operation linked up with socialist industry.

The simple restoration of capitalism is impossible, if only for the reason that the proletariat is in power, that large-scale industry is in the hands of the proletariat, and that transport and credit are in the possession of the proletarian state.

Differentiation in the countryside cannot assume its former dimensions, the middle peasants still constitute the main mass of the peasantry, and the kulak cannot regain his former strength, if only for the reason that the land has been nationalised, that it has been withdrawn from circulation, while our trade, credit, tax and cooperative policy is directed towards restricting the kulaks' exploiting proclivities, towards promoting the welfare of the broad mass of the peasantry and levelling out the extremes in the countryside. That is quite apart from the fact that the fight against the kulaks is now proceeding not only along the old line of organising the poor peasants against the kulaks, but also along the new line of strengthening the alliance of the proletariat and the poor peasants with the mass of the middle peasants against the kulaks. The fact that the opposition does not understand the meaning and significance of the fight against the kulaks along this second line once more confirms that the opposition is straying towards the old path of development in the countryside—the path of capitalist development, when the kulaks and the poor peasants constituted the main forces in the countryside, while the middle peasants were "melting away."

Co-operation is a variety of state capitalism, says the opposition, citing in this connection Lenin's pamphlet *The Tax in Kind*[33]; and, consequently, it does not believe it possible to utilise the co-operatives as the main foothold for socialist development. Here, too, the opposition commits a gross error. Such an interpretation of co-operation was adequate and satisfactory in 1921, when *The Tax in Kind* was written, when we had no developed socialist industry, when Lenin conceived of state capitalism as the possible basic form of conducting our economy, and when he considered co-operation in conjunction with state capitalism. But this interpretation has now become inadequate and has been rendered obsolete by history, for times have changed since then: our socialist industry has developed, state capitalism never took hold to the degree expected, whereas the co-operatives, which now have over ten million members, have begun to link up with socialist industry.

How else are we to explain the fact that already in 1923, two years after *The Tax in Kind* was written, Lenin began to regard co-operation in a different light, and considered that "co-operation, under our conditions, very often entirely coincides with socialism" (see Vol. XXVII, p. 396).

How else can this be explained except by the fact that during those two years socialist industry had grown, whereas state capitalism had failed to take hold to the required extent, in view of which Lenin began to consider co-operation, not in conjunction with state capitalism, but in conjunction with socialist industry?

The conditions of development of co-operation had changed. And so the approach to the question of co-operation had to be changed also.

Here, for instance, is a remarkable passage from Lenin's pamphlet *On Co-operation* (1923), which throws light on this matter:

"*Under state capitalism*, co-operative enterprises differ from state capitalist enterprises, firstly, in that they are private enterprises and, secondly, in that they are collective enterprises. *Under our present system*, co-operative enterprises differ from private capitalist enterprises because they are collective enterprises, but they *do not differ* from socialist enterprises if the land on which they are situated and the means of production belong to the state, i.e., the working class" (see Vol. XXVII, p. 396).

In this short passage two big questions are solved. Firstly, that "our present system" is not state capitalism. Secondly, that co-operative enterprises taken in conjunction with "our system" "do not differ" from socialist enterprises.

I think it would be difficult to express oneself more clearly.

Here is another passage from the same pamphlet of Lenin's:

". . . for us, the mere growth of co-operation (with the 'slight' exception mentioned above) is identical with the growth of socialism, and at the same time we must admit that a radical change has taken place in our whole outlook on socialism" (*ibid.*).

78

Obviously, the pamphlet *On Co-operation* gives a new appraisal of the co-operatives, a thing which the "New Opposition" does not want to admit, and which it is carefully hushing up, in defiance of the facts, in defiance of the obvious truth, in defiance of Leninism. Co-operation taken in conjunction with state capitalism is one thing, and co-operation taken in conjunction with socialist industry is another.

From this, however, it must not be concluded that a gulf lies between The *Tax in Kind* and *On Co-operation*. That would, of course, be wrong. It is sufficient, for instance, to refer to the following passage in The *Tax in Kind* to discern immediately the inseparable connection between The *Tax in Kind* and the pamphlet *On Co-operation* as regards appraisal of the co-operatives. Here it is:

"The transition from concessions to socialism is a transition from one form of large-scale production to another form of large-scale production. The transition from small-proprietor co-operatives to socialism is a transition from small production to large-scale production, i.e., it is a more complicated transition, but, if successful, is capable of embracing wider masses of the population, is capable of pulling up the deeper and more tenacious roots of the old, *pre-socialist* and even pre-capitalist relations, which most stubbornly resist all 'innovations'" (see Vol. XXVI, p. 337).

From this quotation it is evident that even during the time of The *Tax in Kind*, when we had as yet no developed socialist industry, Lenin was of the opinion that, *if successful*, co-operation could be transformed into a powerful weapon in the struggle against "pre-socialist," and, hence, against *capitalist relations*. I think it was precisely this idea that subsequently served as the point of departure for his pamphlet *On Co-operation*.

But what follows from all this?

From all this it follows that the "New Opposition"

approaches the question of co-operation, not in a Marxist way, but metaphysically. It regards co-operation not as a historical phenomenon taken in conjunction with other phenomena, in conjunction, say, with state capitalism (in 1921) or with socialist industry (in 1923), but as something constant and immutable, as a "thing in itself."

Hence the mistakes of the opposition on the question of co-operation, hence its disbelief in the development of the countryside towards socialism through co-operation, hence its turning back to the old path, the path of capitalist development in the countryside.

Such, in general, is the position of the "New Opposition" on the practical questions of socialist construction.

There is only one conclusion: the line of the opposition, so far as it has a line, its wavering and vacillation, its disbelief in our cause and its consternation in face of difficulties, lead to capitulation to the capitalist elements of our economy.

For, if NEP is mainly a retreat, if the socialist nature of state-industry is doubted, if the kulak is almost omnipotent, if little hope can be placed in the co-operatives, if the role of the middle peasant is progressively declining, if the new path of development in the countryside is open to doubt, if the Party is almost degenerating, while the revolution in the West is not very near—then what is there left in the arsenal of the opposition, what can it count on in the struggle against the capitalist elements in our economy? You cannot go into battle armed only with "The Philosophy of the Epoch."[34]

It is clear that the arsenal of the "New Opposition," if it can be termed an arsenal at all, is an unenviable one. It is not an arsenal for battle. Still less is it one for victory.

It is clear that the Party would be doomed "in no time" if it entered the fight equipped with such an arsenal; it would simply have to capitulate to the capitalist elements in our economy.

That is why the Fourteenth Congress of the Party was absolutely right in deciding that "the fight for the victory of socialist construction in the U.S.S.R. is the main task of our Party"; that one of the necessary conditions for the fulfilment of this task is "to combat disbelief in the cause of building socialism in our country and the attempts to represent our enterprises, which are of a 'consistently socialist type' (*Lenin*), as state capitalist enterprises"; that "such ideological trends, which prevent the masses from adopting a conscious attitude towards the building of socialism in general and of a socialist industry in particular, can only serve to hinder the growth of the socialist elements in our economy and to facilitate the struggle of private capital against them"; that "the congress therefore considers that wide-spread educational work must be carried on for the purpose of overcoming these distortions of Leninism" (see Resolution on the Report of the Central Committee of the C.P.S.U.(B.)[35]).

The historical significance of the Fourteenth Congress of the C.P.S.U.(B.) lies in the fact that it was able radically to expose the mistakes of the "New Opposition," that it rejected their disbelief and whining, that it clearly and precisely indicated the path of the further struggle for socialism, opened before the Party the prospect of victory, and thus armed the proletariat with an invincible faith in the victory of socialist construction.

January 25, 1926

Notes

1. See J. V. Stalin, *Works*, Vol. 6, pp. 71-196.

2. See V. I. Lenin, *Works*, 4th Russ. ed., Vol. 22, pp. 173-290.

3. See V. I. Lenin, *Works*, 4th Russ. ed., Vol. 25, pp. 353-462.

4. See V. I. Lenin, *Works*, 4th Russ. ed., Vol. 28, pp. 207-302.

5. See V. I. Lenin, *Works*, 4th Russ. ed., Vol. 31, pp. 1-97.

6. See J. V. Stalin, *Works*, Vol. 6, p. 126.

7. See J. V. Stalin, *Works*, Vol. 6, p. 107.

8. See J. V. Stalin, *Works*, Vol. 6, pp. 395-96.

9. See Karl Marx and Frederick Engels, *The First Address of the Central Committee to the Communist League* (*Selected Works*, Vol. I, Moscow 1951, pp. 99-108).

10. See J. V. Stalin, *Works*, Vol. 6, pp. 379-80.

11. See J. V. Stalin, *Works*, Vol. 6, pp. 185-86.

12. The Second Congress of the Communist International was held July 19-August 7, 1920. J. V. Stalin is here quoting from Lenin's speech on "The Role of the Communist Policy."

13. See V. I. Lenin, *Works*, 4th Russ. ed., Vol. 32, p. 76

14. Tsektran—the Central Committee of the Joint Union of Rail and Water Transport Workers—was formed in September 1920. In 1920 and in the beginning of 1921, the leadership of the Tsektran was in the hands of Trotskyists, who used methods of sheer compulsion and dictation in conducting trade-union activities. In March 1921 the First All-Russian Joint Congress of Rail and Water Transport Workers expelled the Trotskyists from the leadership of the Tsektran, elected a new Central Committee and outlined new methods of trade-union work.

15. See V. I. Lenin, *Works*, 4th Russ. ed., Vol. 32, pp. 1-22

16. The theses of the Second Congress of the Comintern on "The Role of the Communist Party in the Proletarian Revolution" were adopted as a resolution of the congress (for the resolution, see V. I. Lenin, *Works*, 3rd Russ. ed., Vol. XXV, pp. 560-66).

17. See J. V. Stalin, *Works*, Vol. 6, p. 109.

18. See J. V. Stalin's pamphlet, *Lenin and Leninism*, 1924, p. 60

19. See V. I. Lenin, *Works*, 4th Russ. ed., Vol. 33, pp. 427-35

20. For the resolution of the Fourteenth Party Conference on "The Tasks of the Comintern and the R.C.P.(B.) in Connection with the Enlarged Plenum of the E.C.C.I.," see *Resolutions and Decisions of C.P.S.U. Congresses, Conferences and Central Committee Plenums*, Part II, 1953, pp. 43-52.

21. See J. V. Stalin, *Works*, Vol. 7, pp. 111, 120-21.

22. See J. V. Stalin, *Works*, Vol. 7, pp. 111, 117-18.

23. See J. V. Stalin, *Works*, Vol. 7, p. 120.

24. See J. V. Stalin, *Works*, Vol. 7, pp. 267-403.

25. This refers to the plenum of the Central Committee of the R.C.P.(B.) which was held April 23-30, 1925. The plenum endorsed the resolutions adopted by the Fourteenth Conference of the R.C.P.(B.), including the resolution on "The Tasks of the Comintern and the R.C.P.(B.) in Connection with the Enlarged Plenum of the E.C.C.I." that defined the Party's position on the question of the victory of socialism in the U.S.S.R. (See *Resolutions and Decisions of C.P.S.U. Congresses, Conferences and Central Committee Plenums*, Part II, 1953, pp. 43-52.)

26. See *Resolutions and Decisions of C.P.S.U. Congresses, Conferences and Central Committee Plenums*, Part II, 1953, pp. 49 and 46.

27. This refers to the Fourteenth Conference of the R.C.P.(B). held April 27-29, 1925.

28. The reply of the Moscow Committee of the R.C.P.(B.) to the letter of the Twenty-Second Leningrad Gubernia Party Conference, a letter that was a factional attack by the followers of Zinoviev and Kamenev, was published in *Pravda*, No. 291, December 20, 1925.

29. See *Resolutions and Decisions of C.P.S.U. Congresses, Conferences and Central Committee Plenums*, Part II, 1953, p. 77.

30. See J. V. Stalin, *Works*, Vol. 6, pp. 137-38, 140, 141.

31. See V. I. Lenin, *Works*, 4th Russ. ed., Vol. 33, p. 428.

32. See *Resolutions and Decisions of C.P.S.U. Congresses, Conferences and Central Committee Plenums*, Part II, 1953, p. 78.

33. See V. I. Lenin, *Works*, 4th Russ. ed., Vol. 32, pp. 308-43.

34. "The Philosophy of the Epoch" was the title of an anti-Party article written by Zinoviev in 1925. For a criticism of this article, see J. V. Stalin, *Works*, Vol. 7, pp. 385-88.

35. See *Resolutions and Decisions of C.P.S.U. Congresses, Conferences and Central Committee Plenums*, Part II, 1953, p. 75, 77.